Planning for Success

Also available from Continuum

100 Ideas for Lesson Planning – Anthony Haynes

Lesson Planning (3rd edition) – Graham Butt

Planning for Success

Effective Teaching and Learning Methods

Reggie Byram and Hope Dube

continuum

Continuum International Publishing Group
The Tower Building   80 Maiden Lane
11 York Road   Suite 704, New York
SE1 7NX   NY 10038

www.continuumbooks.com

British Library Cataloguing-in-Publication Data
A catalogue record for this book is available from the British Library.

ISBN: 9781847063007 (paperback)

Library of Congress Cataloguing-in-Publication Data
Byram, R. S.
Planning for success : effective teaching and learning methods /
Reggie Byram and Hope Dube.
p. cm.
Includes bibliographical references and index.
ISBN 978-1-84706-300-7
1. Lesson planning. 2. Effective teaching. I. Byram, H. L. (Hope L.)
II. Title.

LB1027.4.B97 2008
371.3'028--dc22

2008019540

Typeset by Newgen Imaging Systems Pvt Ltd, Chennai, India
Printed and bound in Great Britain by MPG Books, Cornwall

Contents

Introduction

The central purpose of this book is to be descriptive and practical. The teacher as planner is, or should be, a part of every course for teachers and trainers.

With all the changes in education and training over the past two or three decades – changes that some teachers have found difficult to comprehend, and managers have come to fear – one thing is certain: the distinctions between education and training have become blurred. Many of these distinctions were never genuine – they were matters of status rather than of education – but they existed nevertheless. Thus, a lecturer in a university was considered to have higher status than an instructor in the craft section of a technical college, while someone who worked in a college of further education and referred to themselves as lecturers might well be accused of putting on airs. The same applied to subject divisions: pure maths was considered to have higher status than applied maths. Older universities were in some way considered *better* than *redbrick* universities. These odious distinctions were the results of class divisions. We know of one university professor who, when asked socially what his occupation was, always referred to himself as a *teacher*, and was proud of the appellation. Invariably he was then asked: 'At which school?' and the answer was: 'The School of Education.'

We have decided to use the term *teacher* throughout, irrespective of the institution or course. In the same way, and for the same reasons, we have used the neutral term *learner* for pupil, learner or trainee. We have no interest in prestige and welcome the blurring of the edges, even the destruction of boundaries in matters related to learning. This is not to say that we think understanding astrophysics is as easy as learning how to make a brick. That would be nonsense. It is, however, a declaration that all forms of learning have worth.

Until quite recently, training was defined as the acquisition of behaviours, which also involved facts and ideas within an occupational context. Education, on the other hand, was person-orientated, rather than occupation-centred. Training implied a large measure of uniformity while education celebrated individual variability. This was largely a product of thinking in the 18th and 19th centuries. Originally, of course, universities were intended to be occupation-centred, producing people, usually men, for the law, the church and the civil service. Now, and not least since polytechnics in Britain were *upgraded* to the status of universities in 1992, the barriers have become more blurred.

Planning works at several levels – long term for a school year, medium term as a series of topics for a semester, and short term detailed notes for a single lesson or series of lessons. The preparation for all cannot be the same.

Much of a trainee teacher's time is taken up with planning lessons – writing out a plan on a piece of paper (or, more likely nowadays, printing out from a computer), having it checked by an experienced teacher and then going through the very useful processes of revision and refinement. Do not be beguiled into believing that experienced teachers do not plan. They do. It is simply that they can do it faster.

Planning involves the statement of long-term aims and short-term objectives. A formal lesson plan establishes goals (objectives) for each teaching session, ensures that appropriate content is included, and provides a feasible timeline. (Time and planning cause considerable anguish to trainee teachers, but getting it right and to time comes with experience.) Your lesson plan also acts as a prompt, and all teachers, experienced or not, need prompts from time to time. The lesson plan, as we shall discover, assists all teachers in maintaining the pace of a lesson. Quite often, pace is a central factor in maintaining the interest of the learner and thus holding attention. Put it another way: planning, at whatever level, helps in focusing the mind of the teacher.

In any job, trade, profession – again, we are back to often unnecessary distinctions – experience brings confidence. Little wrinkles are learned; the best way of doing something is noted; and what is appropriate to a situation is understood implicitly. This is what is meant by *know-how*. Watch a carpenter working with an apprentice. See how the carpenter cuts corners and yet does not produce shoddy work. See how quickly a task is completed and quality maintained. The answer is obvious: the experienced person has done this series of tasks many times before. The apprentice will learn with time. What is true of carpentry is true also of teaching. This does not mean, however, that all we have to do is sit back and with the passage of time expertise will descend on us. The passage of time is the space for learning to plan and learning from our successes and our failures. As we shall discover, failure is not something that should cause distress or anxiety. Rather, it is something from which we can learn.

Experienced teachers have a repertoire of standard lesson segments they are able to draw on in planning and delivering lessons. Some people have claimed that the lack of a formal written plan allows the experienced teacher to respond instinctively to learners' needs during a lesson and change course accordingly. We do not agree with this contention. Such changes can be made even with a lesson plan; there must always be allowance for the contingent and the unforeseen. A plan is an aid to teaching, not a piece of sacred scripture that must not be altered. And as even experienced actors sometimes forget their lines and need a prompt, so all teachers need a plan.

Be aware that good planning will not automatically lead to success in learning. A lesson or series of lessons has to be delivered. However, you can be certain that lack of planning will lead to failure.

1   Effective planning

Aims

There have been several attempts to define what aims are, and in some cases what they should be. Examples are

- A statement of general intent
- A broad statement of what is to be achieved
- A teacher's starting point
- A statement of possible outcomes
- A signpost to what is to be taught and learned

The fact is that teachers do not usually have to devise their own set of aims. This has been done at national level or regional level. Some people complain that there is too much central dictation for teachers. This is not the place to debate that contention. However, it must be stated that teachers have always been constrained by the demands of external factors such as examinations. What the examiner will test, dictates what you must teach. A main aim has always been to complete the syllabus.

A common cause of argument has long been what the purpose of education is. That should be in the plural really: learning has several purposes. The question has been debated in print and on platforms ever since governments legislated for general education.

For some people the aim of education is to strengthen the economy of a country by preparing a cadre of people who can perform successfully a variety of jobs. This we might call the utilitarian view of education, the individual as citizen. Others will enter a strong note of dissent and maintain that education's aim is the development of individuals; personal development that contains within it social skills, academic skills and even spiritual development.

We think there is a place for both. An individual can be prepared by formal learning to be an attorney, a teacher, a motor vehicle mechanic, a worker in an office, or whatever. Within this formal learning will be the skills of literacy and numeracy, and these, properly honed, will allow that person to read novels, appreciate films and conduct themselves as individuals within the broader society and not merely as cogs in an uncomprehending machine.

Curriculum plans change in order to meet the shifting needs of the national economy. Look at the reams of paper produced by central governments. Read them and you will soon discover that they are not radically different from earlier plans; they are a refinement, merely. Quite often things discarded years ago return, but under a different name. There is a proverb in French: '*Plus ca change, plus c'est la même chose*'. It means, 'The more things change, the more they stay the same'. Or, as we might say – What goes round, comes round.

The government of Britain has stated as its general aims that children

- stay healthy and safe;
- secure an excellent education;
- reach the highest possible standards of achievement;
- enjoy their childhood;
- make a positive contribution to society and the economy;
- have lives full of opportunity, free from the effects of poverty.

No sensible teacher would disagree with those six aims. If you do, ask yourself why you entered teaching, and why you remain in it. By the same token, no sensible teacher believes they can all necessarily be achieved, and certainly not by teachers alone. So we are reminded that we are part of a team, part of a region, part of the nation. 'No man,' as John Donne memorably wrote, 'is an island entire unto itself.'

Objectives

Objectives are narrower and more specific than aims. An objective is a target, something to aim for, a goal, a statement of what we hope to achieve in a lesson or a series of lessons.

It is not only teachers who need to consider and then state their objectives. In a general sense we do this all our lives. In many business organizations, people are asked to write work objectives – for themselves and for others – as part of their company's performance planning, training needs assessment and appraisal process. For some, this is a new and difficult experience.

The difficulties are largely imaginary. Thick books with convoluted arguments have been written and published on the subject of what is or is not an objective. Some of these books have often been intemperate in tone. Forget them. Keep it simple.

Ask yourself questions:

- What are learners expected to learn in a certain period of time?
- What is the nature of the work?
- Are different tasks within the period likely to lead to success?
- Learning a set of facts, performing a task at a work bench, understanding and using a computer keyboard, reading a poem or a passage of prose – these objectives, and the means to achieve them, can all be stated. If it can be done, it can be stated. And simply, too.

There are two levels of objective: general and specific.

A *general objective* is an instructional statement followed by a number of anticipated outcomes.

A *specific objective* is concerned with one item of behaviour. A specific objective states what it is the learner will be able to do at the end of the period of instruction. The focus here is narrow; relates directly to a learner's attainment. Close connections with other areas of knowledge and skills is not necessary for the duration of tackling the specific objective. Obviously there are connections: we are talking about close connections. A learner who is seeking to understand a poem must be able to read. A learner shaping a dovetail joint must be able to use a chisel effectively. These other abilities are not – we repeat – not to be learned during the tackling of the objective. Therefore, they do not have to be stated in the lesson plan.

If you are unsure which is a general objective and which a specific objective, consider the language used in the statement. There is a clear difference. A general objective is likely to use the passive voice of verbs. Examples are

At the end of the period, the learner is able to understand . . .
At the end of the period, the learner will be able to apply . . .

With a specific objective, on the other hand, the verb used is usually in the active voice. Examples of active verbs are many: write, fix, change, operate, select, etc. The actual behaviour of the learner is important. This explains why specific objectives are often known as behavioural objectives.

Unfortunately, the term behavioural has sometimes been considered to be the same as behaviourist. This is not so! We have more to say about Behaviourism in Section 2, where we deal with theories of motivation. For the moment, let us simply state that a specific or behavioural objective refers to the learner's behaviour. By behaviour in this context we are not referring to how a learner conducts himself or herself during a period of time. We are not, in other words, thinking about *good behaviour* and *bad behaviour.*

By behaviour, in this context, we mean the actions or reactions of an organism, usually in relation to the environment. Behaviour can be conscious or unconscious, voluntary or involuntary. After we have eaten, food is digested. We are not conscious of these actions, but they are happening, and are behaviour. Such behaviour is controlled by the nervous and endocrine systems – in other words, by electrical and chemical stimuli. The complexity of any behaviour of an organism is related to the complexity of its nervous system. Generally, organisms with complex nervous systems – such as human beings – have a greater capacity to learn new responses and thus adjust their behaviour.

When we state an objective, and set about ensuring the learning of that objective, we seek to change behaviour. Before the lesson, I cannot make a dove-tail joint. After appropriate instruction and practice, I make many dove-tail joints.

You may hear about process or expressive objectives. We prefer the term process, because they state a process the learner undergoes.

The process is more important than the outcome or result. Process objectives are particularly useful in activities such as

- Group work and cooperation
- Analysis of a problem
- Seeking solutions to problems
- Transferring knowledge from one context to another
- Transferring skills from one context to another
- Communications at places of work or learning

These processes overlap, as you can see. They are all process objectives.

Competencies

Competence is the ability to perform an activity to a prescribed standard. The term is used often in an occupational context but is now also applied to other areas of learning.

In 1986 the British government set up the National Council for Vocational Qualifications (NCVQ) and the competencies and levels decided upon by this council became the standard for many other countries too, not least Anglophone countries. In 1997 the National Council became the Qualifications and Curriculum Authority (CQA). There are some differences, but they are differences of emphasis, for the most part, rather than differences of substance. CQA attempts to equate its levels with those of other examination boards., with, for example, level two comparable to General Certificate of Secondary Education (GCSE), level three to Advanced level and level five comparable to professional qualifications of different kinds. A major difference is that vocational qualifications are not awarded after a certain period of time has elapsed – that is, on the basis of time served – but on the successful completion of on-the-job competence or performance. Whatever the name of the authority, whatever the country, vocational qualifications are concerned with competence in work-related tasks. Put another way: qualifications reflect the skills and knowledge needed to do a job effectively.

To begin with, there were four levels, but a fifth came into operation later.

The five levels are:

Level one
Competence that involves the application of knowledge in the performance of a range of varied work activities, most of which are routine and predictable.

Level two
Competence that involves the application of knowledge in a significant range of varied work activities, performed in a variety of contexts. Some of these activities are complex or non-routine and there is some individual responsibility or autonomy. Collaboration with others, perhaps through membership of a work group or team, is often a requirement.

Level three
Competence that involves the application of knowledge in a broad range of varied work activities performed in a wide variety of contexts, most of which are complex and non-routine. There is considerable responsibility and autonomy and control or guidance of others is often required.

Level four
Competence that involves the application of knowledge in a broad range of complex, technical or professional work activities performed in a variety of contexts and with a substantial degree of personal responsibility and autonomy. Responsibility for the work of others and the allocation of resources is often present.

Level five
Competence that involves the application of a range of fundamental principles across a wide and often unpredictable variety of contexts. Very substantial personal autonomy and often significant responsibility for the work of others and for the allocation of substantial resources features strongly, as do personal accountabilities for analysis, diagnosis, design, planning, execution and evaluation.

The central purpose of the changes was to produce a flexible, adaptable and competent work force. Old industries were in decay, or dead. Britain, for example, was in terminal industrial decline as far as traditional manufacturing was concerned. New fields of occupation, not least computer skills, required re-training in order to produce a competent work force.

Elements

A coherent group of elements make up a competence and that competence has to have meaning and independent value in the area of employment to which the award relates. Elements and competencies are determined and endorsed by an industry Lead Body. These Lead Bodies were established in Britain in 1991, to bring a measure of order into a diverse field. Older bodies such as BTEC and RSA continued to offer qualifications but now did so within the framework of the NCVQ and later CQA. This was a radical departure and emanated chiefly from the Dearing Report of 1997, a national committee of inquiry into higher education in Britain.

It is necessary to have elements as sub-units within a unit of competence. An element is something a person in a given occupational area should be able to do. For example, a worker in an office using computers should be able to understand the keys on a QWERTY keyboard. A person fastening metal sheets together has to demonstrate they can insert rivets into the metal. Thus, a unit of competence and the elements within it reflect workplace activity and is worthy of certification as a credit that with other credits leads eventually to an award.

Within each competence there are usually four elements. They are essentially behavioural or specific objectives, in that each is small in range and each is an activity.

Elements as sub-units of a competence can be applied to all levels of work. On a course for managers, for example, we might find the following:

Element G 1: 2   Make contributions to meetings

Work activities
- contributes to team meetings;
- reviews the team meeting;
- contributes to management meetings;
- makes presentations.

Outcomes
- Contributions you have made to:
- agendas and minutes of meetings;
- videos of meetings you have attended;
- correspondence about meetings.

You may also provide your own spoken or written reports, or statements from others who observed your performance.
Written or spoken reports will describe how you

- influenced the views of individuals and the group;
- provided feedback following meetings;
- formed the groups and how they operated;
- consulted people and established their information needs.

witness testimony reports on your performance from others who attended the meeting in your daily work.

This last point is important. Competence-based Education and Training takes place where a person works, be it an office, a shipyard, a bank, a motor repair garage, a private training company or a cruise ship.

Performance criteria

These are statements used to judge whether a competence has been achieved. Each criterion relates to a specified outcome and a statement of evaluation. The purpose of performance criteria is to relate assessment to the successful achievement of an objective or group of objectives. In other words, performance criteria describe what a learner has to do in order to meet agreed standards.

Competence is achieved through consistently meeting the criteria. Consistency is important in a skilled work force. All the criteria do not have to be met during the achievement of an objective – whenever a function is performed. However, all must be achieved over a given period of time.

All practice, in whatever occupation, needs to be underpinned by a certain amount of knowledge and understanding. Some employers complain that it is difficult to determine these levels because of the nature of external examinations in schools. This controversy need not detain us at the moment.

Performance criteria that relate to knowledge and understanding recognize the following levels:

Basic awareness - limited knowledge and general understanding.

Factual awareness - knowledge at a factual level without any understanding of theories and principles.

Working knowledge - the application of factual knowledge to a particular field of practice.

In-depth knowledge - broad and detailed understanding of any theoretical underpinning of a field of practice.

Critical knowledge - the abilities needed to evaluate and devise approaches to situations.

Assessment of performance criteria is a large subject and will be dealt with later in this section.

Range statements

Range statements are concerned with contexts in which performance criteria are meant to apply. Examples of contexts are physical location, employment contexts; or the equipment that is used.

A range statement must accompany each element. This was stipulated from the beginning by the National Council for Vocational Qualifications.

Range statements indicate to assessors the possible range of applications to which an element applies, and the outcomes. The term outcome refers to a short description of a significant, meaningful milestone of learning that is worth reporting upon and recognizing. The outcome describes what a learner is expected to know or do. In other words, range statements set boundaries.

Because there are many occupations, consideration needs to be given to some or all of the following:

- The type of company or organization;
- Work conditions;
- Work pressures;
- The nature of customers or clients;
- The product or service to be provided to customers;

- The materials to be used to provide a product;
- The equipment or resources available to provide the product or service.

What follows is an example of an element from the occupation of office worker.

UNIT 13

Prepare, Produce and Present Documents Using a variety of Sources of Information.

Element 13:2 Produce and present documents using a keyboard

Performance criteria

Error-free documents of approximately 1500 words are produced, under workplace conditions, from selected material, in two and a half hours.

Selected presentation conveys the information effectively, appropriately and inn accordance with house style.

Spelling, grammar and punctuation are consistent and correct.

The language, style and tone of the finished documents are suited to their purpose.

Work practices are in accordance with legal and regulatory requirements and organizational procedures.

Security and confidentiality of information is maintained.

Work is achieved within agreed deadlines.

Documents are finished for presentation, and appropriate routes determined.

Range statements

Text

Graphics

Tables

Keyboard - any form of keyboard available in the workplace

Integrated and edited material includes: unfamiliar vocabulary, complex grammatical structures; and numerical information

Choice of presentation includes: typeface and character; page size; age layout.

Legal regulatory requirements: statutory and non-statutory.
Knowledge/Understanding
Safe and effective operation of keyboard equipment.
Transcribing sources of information of variable quality.
Business and technical vocabulary.
Grammatical structures.
Organizational and conventional presentational styles and
    formats of documents.
Use of dictionaries, reference materials, glossaries.
Paper sizes.
Typeface and character size.
Organization's procedures for the security and confidentiality
    of information.
Relevant legal and regulatory requirements.

Two points will be clear already to the observant reader. First, the fact that competence-based education and training requires a lot of paper to be used. Second, there are many boxes to be ticked. Adverse criticism has been voiced, at seminars and in books and journals. However, our purpose is to describe and not to adopt positions.

Bloom's taxonomy of educational objectives

Benjamin Bloom (1913–99) was an influential American academic educational psychologist, a teacher and researcher at the University of Chicago. Discussions during the 1948 Convention of the American Psychological Association led Bloom to set up a group of educators to undertake the ambitious task of classifying educational goals and objectives. Their intention was no less than to develop a method of classification for thinking behaviours that were believed to be important in the processes of learning. Eventually, this framework became a taxonomy of three domains:

1.   The cognitive domain: concerned with mental skills, knowledge, intellectual outcomes;
2.   The affective domain: concerned with feelings and emotions, interests and attitudes;

3. The psycho-motor domain: concerned motor skills, manual and physical abilities, skills such as swimming, horse riding, keyboard skills, handwriting, the operation of machines.

It has been the cognitive domain which has received most attention and in the view of many teachers has been the most important contribution to education. Important both to the processes of learning and to the measurement of success.

Bloom was a prolific author and his most significant contribution to education is to be found in *Taxonomy of educational objectives*, (1956). A taxonomy, originally used in such areas as botany, means a classification. Bloom created this taxonomy for categorizing levels of abstraction of questions that commonly occur in educational settings. The taxonomy provides a useful structure in which to categorize test questions, and thus be able to devise appropriate strategies for learning.

Bloom's importance and influence lie in his concern with

- mastery learning
- talent development
- a taxonomy of learning, especially in the cognitive domain

Educational objectives were his main, but not exclusive, area of interest. He proposed that any learning task involves at least one of three psychological domains. These are: knowledge, comprehension and analysis. It will now be clear, perhaps, that the National Council for Vocational Qualifications (NCVQ) in Britain, and similar bodies elsewhere, used Bloom's taxonomy closely and effectively in devising strategies for learning and assessment. This is because the taxonomy provides a structure in which learning objectives and learning assessment can be categorized. It was designed to help teachers to classify learning objectives and goals. The foundation of the taxonomy is based on the notion that not all learning objectives and outcomes are the same or of equal value.

In 1956, Benjamin Bloom headed a group of educational psychologists who developed a classification of levels of intellectual behaviour important in learning. Bloom found that over 95 per cent of the test questions that learners encounter require them to think only at the lowest possible level – the recall of information.

Bloom identified six levels within the cognitive domain, from the simple recall or recognition of facts – as the lowest level – through increasingly more complex and abstract mental levels, to the highest order, classified as evaluation.

Verb examples that represent intellectual activity on each level include

> *Knowledge*: arrange, define, duplicate, label, list, memorize, name, order, recognize, relate, recall, repeat, reproduce state.
>
> *Comprehension*: classify, describe, discuss, explain, express, identify, indicate, locate, recognize, report, restate, review, select, translate.
>
> *Application*: apply, choose, demonstrate, dramatize, employ, illustrate, interpret, operate, practice, schedule, sketch, solve, use, write.
>
> *Analysis*: analyse, appraise, calculate, categorize, compare, contrast, criticize, differentiate, discriminate, distinguish, examine, experiment, question, test.
>
> *Synthesis*: arrange, assemble, collect, compose, construct, create, design, develop, formulate, manage, organize, plan, prepare, propose, set up, write.
>
> *Evaluation*: appraise, argue, assess, attach, choose compare, defend estimate, judge, predict, rate, core, select, support, value, evaluate.

Teachers tend to ask most questions from the *knowledge* category. These questions are not poor in themselves, but using them almost exclusively is failing to utilize the higher order question levels. These higher-order questions require much more brain power; they require a more extensive and elaborate answer. Below are the six question categories as defined by Bloom.

1. **Knowledge**
   - remembering;
   - memorizing;
   - recognizing;
   - recalling identification;
   - recall of information.

2. **Comprehension**
   - interpreting;
   - translating from one medium to another;

- o describing in one's own words;
- o organization and selection of facts and ideas.

3. Application
- o problem solving;
- o applying information to produce some result;
- o use of facts, rules and principles.

4. Analysis
- o subdividing something to show how it is put together;
- o finding the underlying structure of a communication;
- o identifying motives;
- o separation of a whole into component parts.

5. Synthesis
- o creating a unique, original product that may be in verbal form or may be a physical object;
- o combination of ideas to form a new whole.

6. Evaluation
- o making value decisions about issues;
- o resolving controversies or differences of opinion;
- o development of opinions, judgements or decisions.

Since the original publication of the first volume, the taxonomy has been refined several times, not least by Bloom himself and his colleagues. The question is: how useful is it for everyday teaching? That the theories are useful starting points for discussion, we have no doubt. But what about the real world of learning? Is it really useful there? We believe that it is a very useful tool, and have used it ourselves in two textbooks. Yes, you may say, but can learners in the early stages tackle such complex skills as analysis and evaluation. We contend that they can, so long as questions are presented in appropriate graded vocabulary and controlled grammatical structures.

In theory, the taxonomy helps teachers better prepare objectives and, from there, derive appropriate measures of learned capability. How far this has been achieved, is open to question. Most curriculum design is handed down to teachers from national or regional bodies and a common complaint is that this national or regional direction inhibits the teacher's ability to set objectives and make original plans. This complaint is not something that need detain us at present.

One important refinement has been the use of verbs rather than nouns. Verbs were deemed to be more appropriate, learners are doing something; that skills are activities in learning. Now we have

- Creating
- Evaluating
- Analysing
- Applying
- Understanding
- Remembering

Planning a scheme of work

It is not likely that you will be called on to devise a syllabus for a course. There are exceptions, of course. You might have been able to persuade someone that you can introduce a new course. We were once in the position of being asked to teach a course in introducing learners to video cameras and their uses, and concluding with learners making their own film. This required a syllabus and schemes before the course could be finally sanctioned.

A scheme is

- Your programme of work;
- Your statement of strategies to be used.

A scheme shows how you expect to cover the syllabus for the course you are teaching.

It is a plan of what will be covered in each week or session of the learning programme or course. It can be very detailed or quite brief, depending on circumstances. A scheme of work may, for example, consider how many lessons will be needed to cover a specific theme.

A scheme of work can also support communication and planning between departments. Once it has been finalised, a scheme of work can be used to write lesson plans. You need to consider the following:

- Allotment of time;
- The content of the course;

- Relationships between sections or modules;
- The background of the learners;
- The skills that learners have acquired already or should have acquired;
- The sequence of presentation;
- Practical work that will be required;
- Special equipment that may be needed.

Your scheme will probably need to be viewed by the head or department or some other person in a position of authority over you. Nevertheless the scheme is not written for that other person. It is your scheme, your plan of action. Its primary importance is for you to be better able to assist the learners.

Your head of department will be less interested, perhaps, in the eight points above than in the following:

- The aims of the full course – your manager will already know these; the point is to show that you are aware of them also.
- The aims of each semester or module.
- The sequence of sessions each week or, in some instances, two week period.
- Teaching methods to be used.
- The activities of the learners in a given period of time.
- Your methods of assessment.
- The position and timing of the methods of assessment.

You will already have noted, being intelligent and thoughtful – the reasons you are or want to be a teacher; the reasons you have chosen to read this book – that there is so far no mention of the material to be learned. The answer is that the material is to be found in the syllabus. Your task is to accept the syllabus and to plan accordingly.

In syllabuses, items are generally placed together in groups or sections according to subject matter. You may, perhaps, wish to prepare lessons in a more appropriate way, a way that aids the learners. Continuity of topic is always important. In a syllabus concerned with Human Biology, for example, one section will deal with the heart and cardio-vascular system, and another, in a different section, with First Aid techniques. A teacher may decide to teach part of the

First Aid – how to deal with and stop haemorrhage – immediately after the series of lessons on the heart and cardio-vascular system. This is one example: you will find many others in your own syllabus.

Be sure always to consider the following:

- The number of lesson periods in a semester;
- The duration of each lesson period;
- Different levels of difficulty in topics;
- Which topics can be related to others;
- Any compulsory topics;
- Any optional topics;
- Those topics most often tested in external examinations;
- How and when you may learn from colleagues;
- How and when you may collaborate with colleagues.

Another nine points, we hear you complain, for you may by now be asking how you can possibly remember them all. There are two pertinent answers. First, you do not have to commit them to memory; they are written down here. And, in addition, they will soon become second nature to you. Trust us! We can vouch for the truth of this from our own experience of many years as teachers at primary and secondary levels, as well as in Further and Higher Education establishments.

Be prepared for the fact that it might not always be possible to complete the syllabus. There are always in life those unforeseen events that no scheme of work, however good, can prepare you for. You may, for example, be absent from work because of your illness or the need for you to care for a loved one during their illness. The chances are that you will be replaced for this period by a succession of supply teachers, and the fact that you have prepared well for those teachers does not ensure success in learning. Or it could be that the establishment has to close down and then shift to another site because of flooding, which neither you nor anyone else could have prevented. In rare cases the school may have been burned down by a disgruntled arsonist who failed external examinations last year or the year before or, more likely, expects to fail this current year. The probable reason for failure to cover all topics is the ability range of the learners. Some may have been admitted to the course without having the necessary background of knowledge and skills, or lack motivation for this particular course. The middle section of this book covers the question of how to motivate learners.

Whatever the reason for failure to complete the syllabus, it is not the end of the world. External examinations boards always include a wide range of topics and your learners will be able to find topics enough, and not be able to claim they have been entered without proper preparation.

It makes sense to prepare only a draft scheme of work. This is much easier now that we all own or have access to computers. Your head of department, or other interested persons, may suggest changes and refinements. You can make these changes on screen much easier than in hard copy. A scheme of work – this bears repetition, because it is important for you to remember it – is a strategic document, not a set of immutable Scriptures. Thus it can be changed. You may also want to make changes yourself. The experience of teaching a course will almost certainly demand that you make refinements.

Here is an actual scheme for Science studies at key stages one and two, primary schools, in England and Wales.

Unit 1A. Ourselves
Unit 1B. Growing plants
Unit 1C. Sorting and using materials
Unit 1D. Light and dark
Unit 1E. Pushes and pulls
Unit 1F. Sound and hearing
Unit 2A. Health and growth
Unit 2B. Plants and animals in the local environment
Unit 2C. Variation
Unit 2D. Grouping and changing materials
Unit 2E. Forces and movement
Unit 2F. Using electricity
Unit 3A. Teeth and eating
Unit 3B. Helping plants grow well
Unit 3C. Characteristics of materials
Unit 3D. Rocks and soils
Unit 3E. Magnets and springs
Unit 3F. Light and shadows
Unit 4A. Moving and growing

Unit 4B. Habitats

Unit 4C. Keeping warm

Unit 4D. Solids, liquids and how they can be separated

Unit 4E. Friction

Unit 4F. Circuits and conductors

Unit 5. Enquiry in environmental and technological contexts

Unit 5A. Keeping healthy

Unit 5B. Life cycles

Unit 5C. Gases around us

Unit 5D. Changing state

Unit 5E. Earth, Sun and Moon

Unit 5F. Changing sounds

Unit 6A. Interdependence and adaptation

Unit 6B. Micro-organisms (short unit)

Unit 6C. More about dissolving

Unit 6D. Reversible and irreversible changes (short unit)

Unit 6E. Forces in action

Unit 6F. How we see things (short unit)

Unit 6G. Changing circuits (short unit)

There then follows a short description of each unit. The following is intended for Unit 1A, Ourselves.

This unit is divided into sections. Each section contains a sequence of activities with related objectives and outcomes. You can view this unit by moving through the sections or print/download the whole unit.

1. Parts of the body
2. The five senses
3. Animals and humans
4. Growing and changing
5. Matching adult and baby animals
6. Growing older
7. Differences between humans
8. How animals move
9. Living and non-living things
10. Eating and drinking

The complete document can be viewed on http://www.standards. dfes.gov.uk/schemes2/science/sci1a, the site of the Department for Children, Schools and Families.

Lesson plans

Your Scheme of Work was a *strategic* plan. Your Lesson Plan is a *tactical* document. The two have much in common. Both should be available for examination, and be capable of being refined in the light of experience. There is an erroneous belief among many teachers that lessons plan are exercises undertaken while in training but need not be done after qualification and getting a post. Or some think lesson planning is a chore for the probationary period, which can be dispensed with afterwards.

There was a time in Britain when a classroom was a teacher's private kingdom. The teacher was generally allowed to get on with working with the learners. There were occasional visits from the Head, who knocked politely, and asked if they might be allowed in. Visits from Her Majesty's Inspectors were even rarer. That privacy and independence began to erode late in the 20th century and has now almost disappeared. The classroom as a private place has gone. It has been transformed. There was never the same measure of autonomy in American schools, but even here there was the central notion that teachers were professional and dedicated people who could be trusted to do the work conscientiously.

It is this matter of trust and privacy that is at the heart of many complaints. When the subject is broached by teachers, it is often in the form of complaints about paperwork, and the burdens that paperwork imposes. Experienced teachers complain they have so much paperwork to complete that they have little time for teaching. Three page lesson plans, special forms for slower learners, especially those struggling to reach national standards for literacy and numeracy, as well as (in some cases) copies of all tests administered, are considered unnecessary, not least because, it is said, few people, if any, ever bother to read these reams of paper. The perception is that lesson plans are printed out by the teacher, are handed in to the office, and disappear into ever burgeoning files. 'Paperwork,

paperwork, paperwork,' is the cry often heard by harassed teachers. In Texas, USA, a state law was enacted known as the Paperwork Reduction Act, limiting the amount of paperwork required of teachers. In some parts of Germany, learners' work is assessed by teaching assistants.

Paperwork and lesson planning are part of a movement to greater control of teachers and what they do. Responding to various criticisms of education, the Prime Minister of Great Britain, James Callaghan, made an important speech in 1976. He compared teaching to a 'secret garden'. In 1988 the decision was made by central government to introduce the national curriculum. In 1993 the Office for Standards in Education (OfSTED) was established. In 2007, OfSTED was merged with the Adult Learning Inspectorate. The effects of these changes meant that instead of inspections every four years or so, more regular visits were carried out. More recently, changes to OfSTED's work have meant inspectors are spending fewer hours in individual classrooms, with the result that inspection reports place greater emphasis on schools' self-evaluation. This means that managers are held responsible for ensuring high quality in teaching. These changes have encouraged managers to monitor their staff more closely.

The emphasis on providing lesson plans is part of a broader transformation aimed at bringing greater openness – or tighter control – to teaching. Either way, lesson planning is now central to a teacher's daily work. If plans are to be useful, they must be truthful. They can in some cases be a retrospective exercise. As some teachers will explain to beginners, 'I write most of my plans after the lesson.' This defeats the whole exercise.

Lesson plans should be prepared in advance and should be available for inspection by colleagues and managers. Teaching has to be made more transparent, the walls or hedges of the secret gardens torn down. School rebuilding has in some cases made classrooms more transparent, literally, with greater use of glass. The increasingly widespread installation of CCTV has made it even easier to monitor lessons. Such surveillance can, of course, be a source of legitimate complaint.

Yet none of these arguments and complaints, however justified, should persuade us that lesson planning is a waste of time, a futile exercise. The burden of preparing lesson plans – if, indeed, it is a burden – has been reduced by the use of computer-generated plans. In some institutions a template or model outline is issued to teachers. This allows for uniformity.

What are the principles of lesson planning?
You need to consider realistic goals for the lesson. Goals that are not too easy; learners need to be stretched. But not goals that are too difficult, which will frustrate learners.

Here is a checklist. Ask these questions.

- What do the learners know already?
- What do the learners need to know?
- What did you do with the learners in the previous class?
- How well do the class work together?
- How motivated are the learners?

What is a lesson plan?
A lesson plan is a framework for a lesson. If you imagine a lesson is like a journey, then the lesson plan is the map. It shows you where you start, where you finish and the route to take to get there.

Essentially the lesson plan sets out what the teacher hopes to achieve over the course of the lesson and how he or she hopes to achieve it. Usually they are in written form but they don't have to be. New or inexperienced teachers may want to or be required to produce very detailed plans – showing clearly what is happening at any particular time in the lesson. However in a realistic teaching environment it is perhaps impractical to consider this detail in planning on a daily basis. As teachers gain experience and confidence, planning is just as important but teachers develop the ability to plan more quickly.

Whatever your level of experience, it is important that all teachers take time to think through their lessons before they enter the classroom.

What should be included in a lesson plan?
Every lesson and every class is different. The content depends on what you want to achieve in a lesson. However it is possible to

make some generalizations. Learners who are interested in, involved in and enjoy what they are studying tend to make better progress and learn faster.

When thinking about a lesson it is useful to keep the following three elements in mind:

1. Engage
2. Study
3. Activate

Engage

This means getting the learners interested in the class. Engaging learners is important for the learning process.

Study

Every lesson usually needs to have some kind of focus. The study element of a lesson could be a focus on any aspect of the language, such as grammar or vocabulary and pronunciation. A study stage could also cover revision and extension of previously taught material.

Activate

Telling learners about the topic is not enough to help them learn it. For learners to develop knowledge and skills, they need to have a chance to produce them.

Why is planning important?

One of the most important reasons to plan is that the teacher needs to identify aims and objectives for the lesson. Teachers need to know what it is they want their learners to be able to do during the lesson and be able to identify skills acquisition at the end of a lesson. In other words: what can learners not do or understand before the lesson began.

Here are some more reasons why planning is important:

- it allows the teacher to predict possible problems and therefore consider solutions;
- it ensures that a lesson is balanced and appropriate for a particular class;
- it gives a teacher confidence from knowing what they are doing;

- it is evidence of good practice;
- it is a sign of professionalism.

It has been said that variety is the spice of life. Variety is certainly the essential spice of teaching, because it is an important means of getting learners engaged and keeping them interested.

Flexibility

No matter how carefully constructed your lesson plan is, no matter how much detail it contains, always expect the unexpected. Things do not always go to plan. Experienced teachers have the ability to cope when things go wrong. It is useful when planning to build in extra and alternative tasks and exercises.

Also teachers need to be aware of what is happening in the classroom. Learners may raise an interesting point and consequent discussion could provide unexpected opportunities for work and practice. In these cases it can be appropriate to branch away from the plan.

Effective lesson planning is the basis of effective teaching. A plan is a guide for the teacher as to where to go and how to get there. However, do not allow the plan to dominate. Be flexible in your planning so that when the opportunities arise you can go, as they say, with the flow.

Do you need to plan if you have a course book?

Many teachers find themselves – for good or ill – having to use a course book. There are advantages and disadvantages to having a course book. Although they do provide a ready-made structure for teaching material, it is very unlikely that the material was written for the teachers' or learners' particular needs. We were teaching in Yemen and were expected to use a course book intended for Australia. The language levels were inappropriate and the cultural content contentious, to say the least. Illustrations of teenagers romping in bikinis on Bondi beach did not rest easily with Muslim parents, many adherents of the Wahhabi sect.

Each class is different and teachers need to be able to adapt material from whatever source so that it is suitable for their learners. A course book can certainly help planning, but it cannot replace the teacher's own ideas of what is suitable for learners, or provide all the material for every lesson. Working through a poor course book has a deadening effect on the teacher and the learners. Even a good course book requires a good source of supplementary material.

Lesson evaluation

Lesson plans always contain a section for an evaluation by the teacher. The space provided can be quite small. Your own evaluation of a learning session is always required. Evaluating the lesson – learner activities, objectives met or not met, your own contribution, is a useful exercise. It is not enough to write 'This was a brilliant lesson!' or 'I was an abject failure!' Something more objective is required.

You need to comment on:

- what the learners have achieved;
- evidence for this achievement;
- the conditions for learning – satisfactory or not;
- behaviour and discipline generally;
- the contribution of support staff;
- whether learners were interested and involved;
- short-term targets for your own improvement.

This needs to be done with each lesson but it does not have to be an onerous task. You can prepare your own template and make copies. A copy can quickly be made for a manager who requests to see it. If you save everything on computer, which we recommend, be sure to have a back-up document, saved preferably on a removable hard disc file. It is galling to lose all records when, as it will one day, your computer crashes. This lesson-by-lesson evaluation will be useful when you consider aspects of evaluation planning.

Evaluation planning

The primary purpose of evaluation is to measure the success of a course or part of a course. You want to know how you are doing, and what and how the learners are doing.

There is a growing awareness that teaching and learning is evidence-based. This means teachers must consider methodology and evaluate that methodology in terms of success or failure of the learners. What you do in class is less important than outcomes stated in terms of learners' performance. The introduction of targets, end of key stage tests and the publication of results, were all clearly intended to raise standards and to tackle underachievement. The teacher is a vital part in these processes.

You can begin your evaluation by asking simple questions. You do not need to subscribe to erudite journals or learn high-flown terminology. You engage in real-life research. You ask questions such as

- What works in the learning process? How and why does it work?
- What does not work? Why does it not work?
- Are the needs of the learners being met? If not, why not?
- How may those needs be better satisfied?
- Do the course materials serve the intended purpose? If not, why not? What improvements, if any, can be made to the material?
- What are the components of your teaching that are worth replicating?

An evaluation will inform you of the success of your planning and thus the success of the activities that you developed for teaching the course. The measures that you defined for your project results and activities serve as the basis for your evaluation. Your evaluation plan should specify the following:

The fundamentals of evaluation

- Structure your evaluation to suit the size and complexity of your project.
- When collecting data, use a combination of methods
- Remember that evaluation is for you.
- Review your data carefully and see if patterns are emerging.
- When you write reports, whether for your own information or for colleagues, mention the following –
  o what has been achieved
  o lessons learned
  o unexpected outcomes

All teaching – and all learning, too – has unintended consequences. We know the truth of this from our own experiences as teachers. Sometimes one can be very surprised indeed. On the national level – in Britain, that is – an unintended consequence of the external publication of results did not always lead to greater moti-vation on the part of managers and teachers. In fact, it has often led to even lower self-esteem on the part of learners with poor achieve-ment levels. The unexpected outcome was de-motivation.

We need to ask what effect such tests have on teaching styles, since we know that the most important influence on achievement is effective teacher planning for learner participation. External tests encourage teaching that transmits knowledge for pupils to learn and reproduce in exams. Teaching and learning too easily become geared to performance in tests, rather than to broader and deeper learning. Learner motivation becomes linked to success in com-petitive exams rather than valuing and understanding the subject being studied. Under pressure to secure good grades, learners may resist opportunities for wider exploration of a topic through read-ing, preferring to stick to precise exam requirements and practice answers. Your evaluation will reveal if this is happening.

The modern classroom should be a creative laboratory, in which a wide repertoire of teaching strategies is drawn upon, stretching each individual to make the maximum progress. In other words, personalisation, focusing on what individuals have learned and under-stood, rather than what parts of the syllabus have been covered.

Growing numbers of teachers are using internal continuous assess-ment of work to find out what learners know and have understood and, therefore, how best to take their learning forward. In other words, assessment *for* learning rather than *of* learning. Continuous formative assessment improves achievement. By making learners active participants in their own learning you will perhaps improve behaviour and motivation, and thus improve learning and perform-ance. Exploration of these issues can lead to forward thinking on your part; what we might call advance evaluation.

Questions are vital. You must always be framing questions, whether about a single period of learning, or about a module. Ask yourself:

- Were the objectives met?
- What feedback is required?
- What form should this feedback take?

- What revision or remedial action is required to assist the learner to move forward?
- How much refinement, if any, does the lesson plan require?
- How does your own evaluation inform future planning?

Teachers, and very often parents too, often conclude that over recent decades there have been too many changes in education. Many feel that a period of stability is needed. Yet nothing stands still. We need to move forward, certainly, but in a planned, coherent way. Planning in evaluation can assist such coherence.

Assessment plans

Assessment is collection, review and use of information about educational courses. It is undertaken in order to measure how far goals have been reached successfully. This means, to measure the learning, performance and development of learners.

In many cases you will have little influence on the types of end-of-course assessment. Usually these will be tests devised by an external examining board. Not all assessment is undertaken at the end of a course, however. Assessment is an ongoing process, and it does not – as we shall discover – always have to be in the form of written tests.

Assessment involves, among many other considerations,

- setting appropriate criteria and standards for learning;
- measurement of success in learning;
- measurement of the quality of learner success;
- gathering evidence of learning outcomes in ways that are fair and reasonable;
- discovering how the performance of learners matches predictions;
- where appropriate, or previously agreed, making the results explicit and public.

The central aim of assessment is to measure the effectiveness of learning and teaching. All data can then be used for making decisions about course changes, course refinement, selection of learners and related criteria.

The first thing to understand is that not all objectives can be fully assessed. Indeed, certain outcomes are only observable many years after a learner has completed a course, and then are hardly amenable to measurement. We are thinking, in this regard, of such areas as the attainment of maturity, of success in interpersonal relations.

To be asked to address a list of 50 learning outcomes – to choose a figure not entirely at random – is possible, but to be asked to assess all 50 is daunting for the teacher, and foolish behaviour on the part of the person who listed the outcomes. Thus, accepting that every outcome cannot be assessed, it is necessary to identify those which are most closely allied to the central purposes of the course. Thus, in a course for nurses it is important to assess techniques for the administering of injections, but not necessary, in this context, to assess the individual's grasp of mathematics. Likewise, in a course designed to choose those learners best fitted to move on to further or higher education, an assessment of how much the learner knows of the Modernist movement is certainly not relevant, especially if the learner is going to continue with science subjects at the next level. Effective assessment demands, therefore, that plans are relevant and manageable. Relevant to the course itself, and manageable by the learner. In other words, planning for assessment requires setting priorities. Avoid trying to measure every possible outcome. This is a waste of your time and the learner's time, but always remember to make clear at the outset what outcomes you intend to measure. The selection will almost always be made from outcomes already agreed by your department or institution.

A selection of assessment methods

Many teachers will immediately think first of classroom tests and of end-of-course examinations. This is natural: these two methods are often bedrock on which all assessment rests. There are, however, alternatives. A few other methods follow.

Case studies

These involve a systematic inquiry into a specific phenomenon: an individual, an event, a particular process or a complete course. Data are collected by way of multiple methods often using both qualitative and quantitative approaches.

Classroom assessment
This is usually designed to improve teaching of a specific course. Data is collected to assess learning outcomes.

Essay questions
In this method, learners are asked to write answers. The questions must be related to course content and agreed levels of outcome.

Objective questioning
In this context, objective means free of subjective bias.

On many courses a battery of objective questions has taken the place of essay writing.

Objective questions, of which we shall have more to say presently, include

- True/false questions
- Yes/no answers
- Multiple choice questions, where usually there are four choices, two of which are wrong, one if almost correct, and only one is completely correct
- Open-ended questions
- Sentences for completion

Embedded questions to assignments
In this technique, questions related to a particular outcome are embedded within course examinations. For example, all sections relating to *research methods* could include a question or set of questions relating to your course learning outcomes. The findings of all learners are analysed and reported in the aggregate.

Exit interviews
Learners leaving the course are interviewed or surveyed to obtain feedback. This already happens in most commercial enterprises. There is no reason why it should not be profitably employed by educational institutions, at whatever level. Data obtained will address the strengths and weaknesses of an institution or course, and the assessment used to make changes where changes are needed.

Content analysis
This is a procedure that categorizes the content of written documents. Analysis begins with identifying the unit of observation – a

word, a phrase, or perhaps a concept – and then creating meaning-ful categories to which each item can be assigned. For example, a learner's statement that 'I discovered that I could be work well with someone from another culture' could be assigned to the cate-gory of Positive Statements about Diversity. The number of times responses of this kind occur can then be quantified and compared with neutral or negative responses addressing the same category.

Collective portfolios

Departments assemble samples of work from learners in various groups or classes and use the collected data to assess specific course learning outcomes. Samples are assessed by using agreed scoring measurements.

Focus groups

Today focus groups are often used by political parties. They also have their uses in educational assessment. Focus groups are planned discussions among homogeneous groups of respondents. It is important that there is a series of carefully constructed open-ended questions. These can be factual questions which then lead on to others about attitudes and experiences. It is useful to record a session and later transcribe the recording for analysis.

Interviews

These are a time-honoured means of assessment, both in business and in education. An interview is a discussion or direct questioning with an individual or group of people. They can be conducted in person but nowadays telephone interviews are being used more frequently. The length of an interview can vary from twenty minutes to over an hour. Interviewers should be trained to follow agreed procedures. Usually interviews are a waste of time and measure very little. Properly constructed and conducted, however, they can be of considerable value.

It will be clear by now, we trust, that as assessment instruments must be chosen to fit circumstances. It is a matter of horses for courses. What is beyond argument is that assessment is necessary. A teacher who does not use assessment techniques ought to start looking for another job.

2 Planning for motivation

Introduction

Motivation goes hand in hand with teaching and learning. What motivates one individual may be very different from what motivates another. Motivation theory is important to the world of work too. As well as individuals, it covers the hopes and aspirations of groups.

Motivation is involved with a number of human characteristics, such as

- determination;
- ambition;
- physical energy;
- intellectual curiosity;
- levels of initiative;
- envy;
- desire – for social approbation, for money, for rank in society;
- passion and love.

The strength or weakness of purpose in an individual or group is what determines levels of motivation. Strength levels are not always consistent.

Psychology is a relatively new discipline. It developed mainly in the 19th century. Like sociology it is a secular discipline that arose to fill the vacuum brought about by the decline of Biblical and religious studies in the face of the rise of science and technology. What had been 'psychology' before the 19th century was generally subsumed within philosophy. The word *psychology* was probably coined by Phillip Melanchthon (1497–1560) in 1653, using two Greek words: breath, spirit or soul and study of. Our modern behavioural sense dates from the last decade of the 19th century.

In 1879, Wilhelm Wundt opened a laboratory at Leipzig University in Germany for the study of this new kind of science that even then was becoming known as *psychology*. 11 years later, William James, an American philosopher (brother of the famous novelist Henry James,) published *Principles of Psychology*, a seminal work which laid the foundations for many of the questions that psychologists would focus on for decades to come. Other important early contributors to the field include Hermann Ebbinghaus, a pioneer in the experimental study of memory at the University of Berlin; and the Russian physiologist Ivan Pavlov who investigated the learning processes now referred to as *classical conditioning*.

Meanwhile, during the 1890s, the Austrian physician Sigmund Freud, who was trained as a neurologist and had no formal training in experimental psychology, started to develop a method of psychotherapy known as psychoanalysis. Freud's understanding of the mind was largely based on interpretative methods and introspection, and was focused in particular on resolving mental distress and treating psychopathology. Freud's theories became very well-known, largely because they tackled subjects such as sexuality, repression and the unconscious mind as general aspects of psychological development. These were largely considered taboo subjects at the time, and Freud provided a catalyst for them to be openly discussed in polite society, or at least among those now termed the *chattering classes*, a pejorative term for the intelligent bourgeoisie Although Freud's theories are of limited (mostly historical) interest to modern academic psychology departments, his application of psychology to clinical work has nevertheless been very influential.

Theories of motivation are crucially important to teachers. It is not necessary to choose to follow one particular school of psychology or one person. An eclectic approach is perhaps the most sensible. However, we cannot choose what is most likely to help us as teachers until we know the various styles and sources. The intention of this section is to present clearly the different strands within educational psychology that are concerned with motivation.

As a teacher or a learner teacher it is likely that you already hold views on the learning process. These may be firmly entrenched. The purpose of this section, as we have stated, is to make you aware of theories and their possible practical applications. It is not our intention to change or even challenge your views, although we may, perhaps, hope to moderate the strictness of some of your conclusions. That said, we have tried to make this section of practical use, for theories by themselves provide no purpose in learning processes.

It is likely that your opinions are a blend of what you have arrived at as a result of what you have read, heard about and observed. In other words, your opinions have been developed from diverse theories on learning, motivation and teaching, largely as a result of your own personal experiences and intellectual development. Thus you may have drawn from behavioural theories, cognitive theories, social cognition theories, attribution theory, achievement motivation theory, as well as using concepts from Piaget or Vygotsky. And not always been aware of the sources, perhaps.

It is not our intention to present a great deal of detail. Rather, we provide you with a short overview of some relevant theories, and you can reach your own conclusions. In the words of T H Huxley − *'Sit down before fact as a little child, be prepared to give up every preconceived notion . . . or you shall learn nothing.'*

Theories of motivation

As you read and as you gain more experience in learning situations − for not all learning occurs in what are generally termed classrooms − you will perceive that there are two main strands − the *cognitive* approach and the *behaviourist* approach. There are many areas where the two approaches overlap. It is not necessary to accept one set to the exclusion of others. The two approaches are presented for the sake of clarity, a quality not always present in textbooks describing educational psychology.

Cognitive approaches

Cognition is a collective term for psychological processes involved in the acquisition, organization and use of knowledge. It was originally meant to indicate the rational side of mental processes, as opposed to those processes driven by emotions. This difference has passed out of use, especially with the development of Artificial Intelligence and computer simulations of human thought processes.

The term is now used to refer to the brain's information processing across a wide range, from such phenomena as memory and attention, to language, thinking and imagery.

Behaviourist approaches

Behaviourism is a term that is widely used, though by some in a narrow way. It is a school of psychology that is concerned only with what is observable and measurable. No account is taken of mental states. Indeed, some behaviourists deny there are such phenomena as mental states. Consciousness and introspection are dismissed, not considered proper areas for study.

As teachers involved in planning to achieve the highest levels of success and effectiveness in our teaching, it behoves us to be clear what motivation is.

We can begin by stating that motivation is an internal state that activates, guides and sustains behaviour. Educational psychology research on motivation is concerned chiefly with learners, and that is how it should be. There are number of factors which are important:

- the volition or will that learners bring to a task;
- levels of interest;
- intrinsic motivation;
- personal goals that guide behaviour;
- beliefs about the causes of success or failure.

To take an example from the fifth point, beliefs about the causes of success or failure. When learners attribute failure to lack of ability – and ability is perceived as uncontrollable – they experience the emotions of shame and embarrassment and consequently decrease effort and show poorer performance. In contrast, when learners attribute failure to lack of effort – and effort is perceived as controllable – they experience the emotion of guilt and consequently increase effort and show improved performance.

Motivational theories also explain how learners' goals affect the way that they engage with academic tasks. Those who have *mastery goals* strive to increase their knowledge. Those who have *performance approach goals* strive for high grades and seek opportunities to demonstrate their skills and abilities. Performance approach goals are generally associated with positive outcomes. Research has produced evidence that mastery goals are associated with many positive outcomes such as persistence in the face of failure, a preference for challenging tasks, as well as creativity and intrinsic motivation.

Those who have performance avoidance goals, however, are driven by fear of failure and avoid situations where perceived weaknesses are exposed. Performance avoidance goals are associated with negative outcomes such as

- poor concentration;
- disorganized studying;
- less self-regulation;
- shallow information processing;
- increased anxiety before any kind of test.

Long before the coining of the term *psychology*, there had been psychologists for many centuries. Most notably, perhaps, Aristotle (384 BC–322 BC). Aristotle was the outstanding Greek philosopher of his times, and his work continued to be influential, especially in Western Europe, for many centuries. In his book *Rhetoric,* Aristotle discusses what today we call motivation. All actions, he states, are due either to reason or to emotion. We seek pleasant things to experience pleasure, and act to avoid unpleasant situations in order to reduce pain. There are seven factors:

1. Chance
2. Nature
3. Compulsions
4. Habit
5. Reasoning
6. Anger
7. Appetite

Chance
Chance events affect us all the time and, although some have little effect in changing what we do, a number of others force us to act or otherwise motivate us into action.

The things that happen by chance are all those whose cause cannot be determined, that have no purpose, and that happen neither always nor usually nor in any fixed way.

Nature
Natural forces are those 'originating in the body, such as the desire for nourishment, namely hunger and thirst' as well as other forces, such as to procreate.

Those things happen by nature which have a fixed and internal cause; they take place uniformly, either always or usually.

Compulsions
Compulsion occurs when we feel that we must act, even though we may not wish to act this way. This may be compliance with the law or dysfunctional obsessive-compulsive behaviour.

Those things happen through compulsion which take place contrary to the desire or reason of the doer, yet through his own agency.

Habit
Habit is unthinking action, and Aristotle said 'Acts are done from habit which men do because they have often done them before.' While compulsion is unpleasant and un-useful repetition of action, habit is pleasant and generally useful.

Habit, whether acquired by mere familiarity or by effort, belongs to the class of pleasant things, for there are many actions not naturally pleasant which men perform with pleasure, once they have become used to them.

Reasoning
Aristotle points out that rational and reasoned action are to defined ends, achieving something that serves personal goals.

Actions are due to reasoning when, in view of any of the goods already mentioned, they appear useful either as ends or as means to an end, and are performed for that reason.

He also notes that when we act in a way that we believe to be rational then we also believe that it is good.

Rational craving is a craving for good, i.e. a wish – nobody wishes for anything unless he thinks it good. Irrational craving is twofold, viz. anger and appetite.

Anger

Sometimes interpreted as 'passion', anger can lead to extreme action. Anger is closely related to the need to revenge, and anger decreases when there is no prospect of vengeance.

To passion and anger are due all acts of revenge . . . no one grows angry with a person on whom there is no prospect of taking vengeance, and we feel comparatively little anger, or none at all, with those who are much our superiors in power.

Aristotle notes that angry people suffer extreme pain when they fail to get their revenge. If we apply Freud's pain-reduction principle, then perhaps it is not surprising that anger reduces in such circumstances.

Appetite

Sometimes interpreted as 'desire', appetite is 'craving for pleasure'.

While anger serves negative motivation, 'Appetite is the cause of all actions that appear pleasant'. Aristotle pointed out that wealth or poverty is not a cause of action, although the appetite for wealth may well motivate.

Nor, again, is action due to wealth or poverty; it is of course true that poor men, being short of money, do have an appetite for it, and that rich men, being able to command needless pleasures, do have an appetite for such pleasures: but here, again, their actions will be due not to wealth or poverty but to appetite

These are all motivations that drive people in different ways, and some people are more affected by certain drives than by others. If we can understand how drives affect people in specific ways, then we may be better able to influence them and motivate them effectively. Obviously, this is nowhere as important as in teaching and learning.

Among modern theories of motivation the first to be considered is Behaviourism.

Behaviourism
Behavioural psychology, also known as behaviourism, is a theory of learning based on the idea that all behaviours are acquired through conditioning. Conditioning occurs as a result of interaction with the environment. According to behaviourists, behaviour can be studied in a systematic and observable manner with no consideration of internal mental states.

Important events in the development of Behaviourism include

1863: Ivan Sechenov's *Reflexes of the Brain* is published. A neurophysiologist, he introduces the concept of inhibitory responses in the central nervous system.
1900: Ivan Pavlov begins studying salivary response and other reflexes.
1913: John B. Watson's *Psychology as a Behaviourist Views It* is published. He outlines many of the main points of behaviourism.
1920: Watson and an assistant conduct the *Little Albert* experiment.
1943: Clark Hull's *Principles of Behaviour* is published.
1948: B. F. Skinner publishes *Walden II* in which he describes in fictional form a utopian society founded on behaviourist principles.
1959: Noam Chomsky publishes his criticism of Skinner's behaviourism, in *Review of Verbal Behaviour*.
1971: B. F. Skinner publishes *Beyond Freedom and Dignity*, where he argues, among other subjects, that free will is an illusion.

Major thinkers and practitioners in the field of Behaviourism include

Ivan Pavlov	(1849–1936)
Edward Thorndike	(1874–1949)
John B. Watson	(1878–1958)
Clark Hull	(1884–1952)
B. F. Skinner	(1904–1990)

Others who are important to the development of Behaviourism are mentioned in later pages and in the Biographical Appendix.

There are **two** types of conditioning:

1. Classical conditioning
2. Operant conditioning

Behaviourism and classical conditioning

Behaviourism is, as we have noted, a school of thought in psychology that assumes learning occurs through interactions with the environment. Environmental stimuli shape all behaviour, and it is largely a waste of time and effort to take into consideration such internal mental states such as thoughts, feelings and emotions. These, if they even exist, are of no use in explaining behaviour.

One of the best-known aspects of behavioural learning theory is *classical conditioning*. This developed from the work of Ivan Pavlov. Classical conditioning is a learning process that occurs through associations between an environmental stimulus and a naturally occurring stimulus. In order to understand how classical conditioning works, it is important to be familiar with the basic principles of the process. It must be remembered that Pavlov was a physiologist, and that he studied animals such as dogs, rather than human interactions. Nevertheless, many of the conclusions apply to human behaviour.

Classical conditioning is a technique used in behavioural training in which a naturally occurring stimulus is paired with a response. Next, a previously neutral stimulus is paired with the naturally occurring stimulus. Eventually, the previously neutral stimulus comes to evoke the response without the presence of the naturally occurring stimulus. The two elements are then known as the *conditioned stimulus* and the *conditioned response*.

Operant conditioning (sometimes referred to as instrumental conditioning) is a method of learning that occurs through rewards and punishments for behaviour. Through operant conditioning, an association is made between a certain kind of behaviour and a consequence for that behaviour.

Let us first learn more about classical conditioning.

The unconditioned stimulus

The unconditioned stimulus is one that unconditionally, naturally and automatically triggers a response. For example, when we smell one of our favourite foods, we may immediately feel very hungry. In this example, the smell of the food is the unconditioned stimulus.

The unconditioned response

The unconditioned response is the unlearned response that occurs naturally in response to the unconditioned stimulus. In our example, the feeling of hunger in response to the smell of food is the unconditioned response.

The conditioned stimulus

The conditioned stimulus is a previously neutral stimulus that, after becoming associated with the unconditioned stimulus, eventually comes to trigger a conditioned response. Suppose that when you smell your favourite food, you also hear the sound of a whistle. While the whistle is unrelated to the smell of the food, if the sound of the whistle is paired multiple times with the smell, the sound eventually triggers the conditioned response. In this case, the sound of the whistle is the conditioned stimulus. Pavlov is famously known to have used the sound of a bell rather than a whistle.

The conditioned response

The conditioned response is the learned response to the previously neutral stimulus. In our example, the conditioned response would be feeling hungry when you heard the sound of the whistle.

In the real world, as opposed to the laboratory, human beings do not respond exactly like Pavlov's dogs. (They behave like dogs and other animals in more ways than some people wish to admit, however.) There are numerous real-world applications for classical conditioning. Many dog trainers use classical conditioning techniques to help people train their pets. Some have used it to train their children. And even some hoping to find success in teaching.

These techniques are useful in the treatment of phobias or other anxiety conditions. Teachers are able to apply classical conditioning in the class by creating a positive classroom environment to help learners overcome anxiety or fear. Pairing an anxiety-provoking situation – such as talking or acting in front of a group – with pleasant surroundings helps the learner develop new associations. Instead of feeling anxious and tense in these situations, the learner becomes more relaxed and calmer.

Behaviourism and operant conditioning

Operant conditioning (sometimes known as instrumental conditioning) is different from Pavlovian or *classical conditioning*, in that the unconditioned stimulus is independent from the behaviour of the animal, and is contingent upon environmental events. It is a system of learning that operates through rewards and punishments for behaviour. An association is made between a behaviour and a consequence for that behaviour.

There are innumerable examples of operant conditioning at work. These include

- children performing household chores on the promise of receiving pocket money;
- children completing homework to earn a reward from a parent or teacher;
- employees completing projects in order to receive praise, promotion or a bonus.

The promise or possibility of rewards causes an increase in behaviour. But operant conditioning can also be used to decrease a behaviour by punishment of some kind, such as the withdrawal of favour or reward.

Among the terms used in behaviourism are
A *reinforcer* is any event that strengthens or increases the behaviour it follows. There are two kinds of reinforcers:

1. positive reinforcers are favourable events or outcomes that are presented after the behaviour.
2. negative reinforcers involve the removal of unfavourable events or outcomes after the display of a behaviour.

Punishment is the presentation of an adverse event or outcome that causes a decrease in the behaviour it follows. There are two kinds of punishment:

positive punishment involves the presentation of an unfavourable event or outcome in order to weaken a response.
negative punishment occurs when a favourable event or outcome is removed after a certain kind of behaviour occurs. Negative punishment is intended to result in a decrease in behaviour.

The major theorists for the development of operant condition-ing are Thorndike, Watson, Clark Hull and Skinner.

Edward Thorndike

Thorndike became a pioneer in comparative psychology after reading William James's *Principles of Psychology* (published 1890) and enrolled at Harvard University in order to study under James. Thorndike's research interest was in how children learn, but his methods precluded their study. So, he developed projects that examined learning in animals. He completed a study of maze learn-ing in chickens. Later, he continued his animal research using cats and dogs. In 1898, he was awarded a doctorate for his thesis, *Animal Intelligence: An Experimental Study of the Associative Processes in Animals*, in which he concluded that an experimental approach is the only way to understand learning.

Among Thorndike's most famous contributions was his state-ment of his Law of Effect:

- responses that are closely followed by satisfying consequences become associated with the situation, and are more likely to recur when the situation is subsequently encountered.
- responses followed by aversive consequences or associations to the situation become weaker.

Thorndike's experiments were motivated in part by his dislike for statements that animals make use of extraordinary faculties such as insight in their problem solving. Animals are, he once said, often quite stupid. His intention was to distinguish clearly whether or not cats escaping from puzzle boxes were using insight. Thorndike's instruments in answering this question were 'learning curves' reve-aled by plotting the time it took for an animal to escape each time it was placed in the box. He reasoned that if the animals showed 'insight', then their time to escape would decrease to a negligible period, which would also be shown in the learning curve as an abrupt drop; while animals using a more ordinary method of trial and error would show gradual curves. His finding was that cats consistently showed gradual learning. He interpreted his findings in terms of *associations*. He asserted that the connection between the box and the motions the cat used to escape was *strengthened* by each escape. (A similar, though radically reworked notion was taken up by B. F. Skinner in his later formulation of operant conditioning.)

Thorndike specified **three** conditions that maximize learning:

1. The law of effect stated that the likely recurrence of a response is generally governed by its consequence or effect generally in the form of reward or punishment;
2. The law of recency stated that the most recent response is likely to govern the recurrence;
3. The law of exercise stated that stimulus–response associations are strengthened through repetition.

Thorndike's conclusions were influential in education for at least fifty years and have adherents even today.

John B Watson

After leaving university, Watson, an American like most of the leading players in the development of behaviourism, went into the advertising business. He wanted to use scientific theories of behaviourism and the emotions of fear, rage and love to improve the effects of advertising on consumers. He also wrote books about controls over human emotions.

In 1920 Watson published his most famous conditioning experiment – the *Little Albert* study – in which he produced, in a small child, conditioned fear of a white rat by repeatedly presenting it paired with the loud clanging sound of a metal bar. This conditioned fear was then shown to generalize to other white furry objects, including a Santa Claus mask and even to Watson's own white hair. In another well-known article, published in 1920, Watson argued that thinking, a mental activity that seems to involve no overt behaviour, is nothing more than sub-vocal speaking, but within a decade he had retracted this extreme view.

In a number of publications (for example, *Behaviour: An Introduction to Comparative Psychology* and *Behaviourism*) Watson states that behaviourism is the scientific study of human behaviour. It is simply the study of what people do. Behaviourism is intended to take psychology to the same level as other sciences. The first task is to observe behaviour and make predictions, and then to determine causal relationships. Behaviour can be reduced to relationships between stimuli and responses, the S/R Model. A stimulus can be shown to cause a response or a response can be traced back to a stimulus. All behaviour can be reduced to this basic component. According to Watson, 'life's most complicated acts are but combinations of these simple stimulus–response patterns of behaviour.'

Among Watson's conclusions are

- Conditioning is the process of learning to react to the environment. Much behaviour has been previously conditioned in the human species by the environment. To gain control of a subject of study the behaviourist must know which behaviours have been preconditioned and which inherited from past generations.
- Human psychology should not be concerned with speculation but with observable facts learned from experiments.
- Examination of states of consciousness is not the concern of the psychologist.
- In other words, Watson wanted the removal of subjectivity from psychology. The findings of psychology can all be explained in physical and chemical terms.

Leonard Clark Hull

Clark Hull studied mining engineering at the University of Wisconsin, and then switched to psychology, finally gaining his doctorate in 1918 at the comparatively late age of thirty-four years. Hull's doctoral dissertation moved experimental psychology into the area of thought processes by investigating the learning of concepts. Although the dissertation was published in a journal, no one appeared to take notice. His interests seemed too wide for narrow academics. And indeed Clark Hull had many interests. He developed methods of statistical analysis. He invented a machine to calculate correlations. He also investigated concept formation, and, perhaps surprisingly, hypnosis and suggestibility.

Then, in 1927, he read Pavlov and this changed his focus. Now he was a behaviourist. He tackled the problems of conditioned reflexes and learning. His major books were *Principles of Behaviour* (1943) and *A Behaviour System* (1952).

He read Isaac Newton's *Principia* (1697) to discover, if possible, where his early efforts at theory had faltered. Any difference between psychology and physics, held Hull, is in degree and not in kind. Psychology was a science and had to use scientific methods. There was no place for notions such as consciousness, purpose or any other mentalist idea. He viewed human behaviour as automatic and reducible to the language and methods of physics. He warned against giving subjective meanings to any behaviour being observed.

For 20 years Clark Hull held a dominant position in American academic psychology. And this at a time when Skinner was active. Vast numbers of experiments by experimental psychologists all across the United States were conducted in order to confirm or challenge his theoretical formulations. Then, almost overnight, his work went out of fashion. A different generation failed to be satisfied with mechanistic views of behaviour; conditioning theory did not have the means to explain motivation convincingly. Hull himself admitted, late in his life, that perhaps behaviourist systems could be applied only to hungry rodents.

Nevertheless, Hull's work has value. He held that

- we should begin with specific testable postulates, even if these are based on minimal evidence;
- from these postulates we derive concrete, empirically verifiable deductions and are able to test them;
- the task of a theorist is to formulate postulates so that they will lead to unequivocal deductions;
- the value of a theory resides in how much research it generates and how consistent with its theoretical deductions the findings are;
- it is necessary to subject theories to constant revision in the light of empirical results.

Perhaps Hull's lasting contribution to experimental psychology was his precision in experimental design. This remains important in all experimental psychology. He also rejected the use of the term *instinct*, which was controversial, and in its place put the term *drive*.

For teachers and learners some of his conclusions are important. They include

- drive is based on an animal's needs: hunger, thirst, sexual arousal, pain;
- drive activates all behaviour;

- reinforcement occurs whenever drive is reduced, leading to learning and the solution of a problem;
- need-related motivation, drive, and S-R learning are produced by reinforcement, and only by reinforcement. The S-R connection is what we know as *habit*.

Clark Hull held that drives can be substituted in motivating behaviour. For example, if a hungry animal has learned a given response to obtain food, it should be easy to transfer the same response to obtain water. Early studies tended to confirm this motivation transfer, but further experiments failed to find sufficient evidence to support this.

An alternative formulation was proposed by Miller and Dollard. Using a similar habit construct, they proposed that any strong stimulus can have motivating or drive properties without being tied to the needs of the organism. Drive and habit act together to determine the strength of behaviour. Strength depends on an animal's motivation at the time of testing and the amount of prior learning. Neither motivation nor prior learning alone will predict what an animal learns in a particular situation.

Miller and Dollard tried to combine the insights provided by Sigmund Freud with scientific rigour, which Freud always conspicuously lacked despite the accumulation of many cases and records. In order to understand human behaviour, we must understand the psychological principles involved in learning and also the social conditions in which learning is expected to take place. A commonplace today, perhaps, but not so obvious to everyone in 1941. Psychology, they declared, describes the learning principles, while the other social science disciplines describe conditions.

Teachers can benefit from some of the conclusions reached by Hull and his associates. Points include

- habit is developed as result of drive reduction
- habit strength depends on 4 independent variables:
- the number of reinforced trials
  - o the magnitude of reward
  - o immediacy or delay in reinforcement
  - o the interval between the conditioned stimulus (CS) onset and the unconditioned stimulus (US)

B. F. Skinner

Skinner was born in Pennsylvania. He attended Hamilton College in New York. His ambition was to become a successful writer of fiction. He received his bachelor's degree in English literature. After graduation, he spent a year attempting to become a writer of fiction, but he became disillusioned and concluded that he lacked enough experience of life. During this time, he read a copy of Bertrand Russell's recently published book *An Outline of Philosophy*, in which Russell discusses the behaviourist philosophy of psychologist John B. Watson. At the time, Skinner had begun to take more interest in the actions and behaviour of those around him, and some of his short stories had taken a psychological slant. He decided to abandon literature and seek admission as a graduate learner in psychology at Harvard University. While a learner, he invented the operant conditioning chamber and cumulative recorder, developed the *rate of response* as a critical dependent variable in psychological research, and also developed a powerful, inductive, data-driven method of experimental research.

After posts in various American universities, Skinner returned in 1948 to Harvard as a professor and remained there for the rest of his career. He wrote many books of which, perhaps, the best known is *Walden II*, a fictional account of a community run on behaviourist principles.

Skinner's theories

Skinner's entire system is based on *operant conditioning*. An organism, whether amoeba or human being, is in the process of operating on the environment. During this operating, the organism encounters a special kind of stimulus, called a *reinforcing stimulus*. Behaviour is followed by a consequence, and the nature of the consequence modifies the organism's tendency to repeat the behaviour in the future. A behaviour no longer followed by the reinforcing stimulus results in a decreased probability of that behaviour occurring in the future.

Skinner claimed that he accidentally (that is, operantly) came across his various discoveries. For example, he talks about running low on food pellets in the middle of a study. He had to reduce the number and frequency of reinforcement pellets. Reinforcement does not have to be continuous. Thus he discovered that there are different *schedules of reinforcement*.

Shaping

A question Skinner had to consider was how we develop more complex levels of behaviours. He responded with the notion of *shaping*, or 'the method of successive approximations.' Basically, this involves first reinforcing a behaviour only vaguely similar to the one desired. Once that is established, you look out for variations that come a little closer to what you want, and so on, until you have the animal performing a behaviour that would never show up in ordinary life. For example, Skinner was successful in teaching simple animals to do some quite extraordinary things such as pigeons being able to play games.

Beyond these fairly simple examples, shaping also accounts for the most complex of behaviours. You do not, for example, become a brain surgeon by stumbling into an operating theatre, cutting open someone's head, successfully removing a tumour and being rewarded with prestige and a hefty pay cheque, along the lines of the rat in the Skinner box receiving food pellets. Instead, you are shaped by your environment to enjoy certain things, do well in school, take a biology class, have a good hospital visit, enter medical school, be encouraged to specialize in brain surgery and so on. Your parents and teachers would no doubt be an influence, giving advice and praise at appropriate times. This could be something your parents were carefully doing to you, as if you were a rat in a cage.

Aversive stimuli

An aversive stimulus is the opposite of a reinforcing stimulus – it is something we find unpleasant or painful. A behaviour followed by an aversive stimulus results in a decreased probability of the behaviour occurring in the future. This both defines an aversive stimulus and describes the form of conditioning known as *punishment*. If you deliver an electric shock to a rat for doing something, it will do a lot less of it in the future. If you spank a child for throwing toys, he will, perhaps, throw his toys less often, for fear of punishment.

Skinner did not approve of the use of aversive stimuli for children. This was not in any way connected with ethical considerations but the observable fact that aversive stimuli do not always work successfully. All teachers know this, or soon learn it.

Behaviour modification

This is a therapy technique based on Skinner's work. It is very straight-forward: extinguish an undesirable behaviour (by removing the reinforcer) and replace it with a desirable behaviour by reinforcement. It has been used on several kinds of psychological problems: addictions, neuroses, shyness, autism and in some cases even schizophrenia. It is particularly successful with children.

Operant conditioning has played a major role in the development of the science of psychology, especially in the United States. This is true of educational psychology too. Learning is the result of the application of consequences; that is, learners begin to connect certain responses with certain stimuli. This connection causes the probability of the response to change, and in this change learning occurs.

The value of behaviourism for teachers is that it is based on *observable* behaviours, and this makes it easier to quantify and collect data and information when conducting research.

Effective therapeutic techniques such as intensive intervention and discrete trial training are all rooted in behaviourism. These approaches are often very useful in changing maladaptive or harmful behaviours in both children and adults.

Behaviourism has its critics, however. Some people argue that it is a one-dimensional approach and that behavioural theories do not account for free will and internal influences such as moods, thoughts and feelings. In addition, behaviourists do not take into account learning that occurs without the use of reinforcements or punishments. Both people and animals are able to adapt their behaviour when new information is introduced, even if a previous behaviour pattern has been established through reinforcement.

Dominant for about fifty years, behaviourism has now been replaced by other theories. Before moving on to these other points, however, it is perhaps worth noting that shaping played a large part in the therapy of *systematic desensitization*, developed by Joseph Wolpe (1915–97) and Arnold Lazarus (born 1932), two South Africans who took American citizenship. A person with a phobia – for example, of spiders – is invited to consider different scenarios involving spiders and panic of one degree or another. The first scenario would be a very mild one, perhaps seeing a small spider at a great distance, and then gradually increase in severity until there is a scenario involving something completely terrifying – say a tarantula climbing on your face while you are driving your car at a hundred miles per hour. Relaxation techniques involving muscles are introduced gradually. There is clearly a place for these techniques in education, especially with learners with phobias, or even those who exhibit various kinds of disruptive behaviour.

Cognitive theories

Cognitive theories first appeared toward the end of the 19th century but were usurped by behavioural theories. Only in the second half of the 20th century did cognitive views return to notice and now they are the dominant force in educational psychology.

These theories are concerned with the mental events that take place as we learn. Unlike the behaviourists, the cognitive theorists accept that learners actively process information by

- organization;
- making new relationships between old knowledge and new learning;
- storage of information.

The learner is not a passive recipient of stimuli but an active organism.

Cognitive theories of educational psychology developed before or contemporaneously with behaviourist theories. However, cognitive theories have only become dominant in the past 50 years or so, as a direct result of dissatisfaction with behaviourism. There was a strengthening of opinion that behaviourists, by omitting mental activity from their considerations, were failing to present the complete picture of learning activities. Cognitivism focuses on both mental knowledge and behaviour.

Although there is considerable diversity among cognitive theorists, the making of a number of general assumptions is possible. These include

- knowledge is organized;
- that some learning processes are unique to human beings;
- learning is a process of relating new information to previously learned information;

- objective and systematic observations of human behaviour are the focus of scientific inquiry;
- inferences about unobservable mental processes can be deduced from behaviour;
- individuals are actively involved in learning processes;
- learning involves the formation of mental associations that are not necessarily reflected in overt changes in behaviour.

The implications of these general assumptions for teaching and learning include:

- that cognitive processes influence learning;
- that as children become older and develop physically, they become capable of higher levels of thought;
- that organization of thoughts leads to learning;
- that new information is most easily acquired when associated with existing knowledge;
- that individuals have the capacity to take control over their own learning.

Jean Piaget

Piaget was born in 1896 in Neuchâtel, Switzerland and lived to 1980. He was interested in philosophy, the natural sciences and developmental psychology. In 1918, Piaget received his Doctorate in Science from the University of Neuchâtel. He worked for a year at psychology laboratories in Zurich and at Eugen Bleuler's psychiatric clinic, where he became acquainted with the work of Sigmund Freud and Carl Gustav Jung. (Like Jung, Bleuler was a follower of Freud who came to disagree with Freud on fundamental matters. He is remembered today as the person who coined the term *schizophrenia*.)

In 1919, Piaget taught psychology and philosophy at the Sorbonne in Paris and conducted research on intelligence testing. He was critical of intelligence tests, which usually demanded a right or wrong answer, and he showed more interest in how children use reason.

By 1921 he was back in Switzerland, as a lecturer at Geneva. Along with colleagues, Piaget started research on the reasoning of elementary school children. This research developed into five books on child psychology. Although Piaget considered this research highly preliminary, he was surprised by the strong positive public reaction to his work.

Piaget provided many central concepts in the field of developmental psychology and the growth of intelligence, which for him meant the ability to more accurately represent the world and perform logical operations and concepts grounded in the world. The theory concerns the emergence and acquisition of schemata— schemes of how people, particularly children, perceive the world – in *developmental stages.*

These stages are times when children are acquiring new ways of mentally representing information. The theory is considered 'constructivist', meaning that it asserts that we construct our cognitive abilities through self-motivated action in the world.

Piaget divided schemes that children use to understand the world through **four** main periods or stages, roughly corresponding to chronological age:

1. Sensori-motor stage   (years 0–2)
2. Pre-operational stage   (years 2–7)
3. Concrete operational stage   (years 7–11)
4. Formal operational stage   (years 11–adulthood)

Sensori-motor stage
This stage is one of using the senses. According to Piaget infants are born with a set of reflexes and a drive to explore their world. (There are six sub-stages but these are not crucially important in motivation planning.)

Pre-operational stage
By observing sequences of play, Piaget was able to demonstrate that towards the end of the second year a new kind of psychological functioning occurs. Children learn to use and to represent objects by images and words. In this stage, also, children develop their language skills. But thinking is still egocentric, self-centred. There is difficulty understanding the viewpoint of others. They still use intuitive rather than logical reasoning. However, the child is able to classify objects by a single feature: for example, grouping together all the red blocks regardless of shape, or all the square blocks regardless of colour.

The main point is that children are unable to understand their place in the world and how they are related to others. They have trouble understanding what emotions of others. But as they mature they grow in their abilities to understand others' perspectives. Children have highly imaginative minds at this time and actually assign emotions to inanimate objects such as dolls and toys.

Concrete operational stage

This stage occurs between the ages of 6 and 12 years and is characterized by the appropriate development and use of logic. Important processes during this stage are

- **Seriation:** this is the ability to sort objects in an order according to size, shape or any other characteristic. For example, if given different-shaded objects they may make a colour gradient.
- **Classification:** the ability to name and identify sets of objects according to appearance, size or other characteristic, including the idea that one set of objects can include another. A child is no longer subject to the illogical limitations of animism (the belief that all objects are alive and therefore have feelings).
- **Decentering:** where the child takes into account multiple aspects of a problem to solve it. For example, the child will no longer perceive an exceptionally wide but short cup to contain less than a wide, taller cup.
- **Reversibility:** where the child understands that numbers or objects can be changed, then returned to their original state. For this reason, a child will be able to rapidly determine that if 4+4 equals 8, 8−4 will equal 4, the original quantity.
- **Conservation:** understanding that quantity, length or number of items is unrelated to the arrangement or appearance of the object or items. For instance, when a child is presented with two equally-sized, full cups they will be able to discern that if water is transferred to another container it will conserve the quantity and be equal to the filled cup.
- **Elimination of egocentrism:** the ability to view things from another's perspective (even if they think incorrectly).

Formal operational stage

This is the fourth and final of the periods of cognitive development in Piaget's theory. This stage develops at around 11 years of age and continues into adulthood. It is characterized by acquisition of the ability to think abstractly, reason logically and draw conclusions from the information available. During this stage the young adult is able to understand such things as love, logical proofs and values. Biological development plays a part for the changes occur during puberty, the period of physical and emotional changes that mark the entry to adulthood. It has to be said that many adults never reach the final stage where reasoning is possible; even as adults they remain within the concrete operational stage.

General observations regarding characteristics of the four stages

- although the timing may vary, the sequence of the stages does not;
- the stages are universal and in no way culturally specific;
- we are able to generalize: the representational and logical operations available to the child should extend to all kinds of concepts and content knowledge;
- stages are logically organized wholes;
- the stages are hierarchical in that each successive stage incorporates elements of previous stages, but is more differentiated and integrated;
- the stages represent qualitative differences in modes of thinking, not merely quantitative differences.

Challenges to the stage theory

Piaget's account of development has not lacked its critics. Criticisms include

- development does not always progress in the smooth manner his theory seems to predict.
- unpredicted gaps in the developmental progression suggest that the stage model is at best a useful approximation;
- while it is predicted that cognitive maturation occurs concurrently across different domains of knowledge (such as

mathematics, logic, understanding of physics, of language), more recent developments have been influenced by trends in cognitive science away from domain generality;

- different cognitive faculties may be largely independent of one another and thus develop according to quite different time-tables;

What is not under challenge is the fact that Piaget changed the emphasis from observable behaviour to mental faculties. In addition, observation and research was conducted with human beings, children and not with laboratory rats, mice and pigeons.

Other cognitive theorists worthy of study include Jerome Bruner, David Ausubel, Robert Gagné and Albert Bandura. Although they have sometimes adopted different theoretical positions, they share the following features in common.

- they all put forward their ideas initially in the 1960s;
- at that time all three were established in their careers and recognized as authorities in their own right;
- all attempted to define cognitive theories of instruction.

The advent of these theories is important because they coincided with a period in which Western educators were, for the first time since the 1920s, seriously able to consider educational policies and institutions. Economic depression and the Second World War had made such evaluations impossible before 1945. Of equal importance was the fact that this period of questioning in the 1960s coincided with unprecedented growth in scientific knowledge. In addition, there was a rapid expansion – in western countries especially, but also in emergent nations – of universal secondary education.

Jerome Bruner

Jerome Bruner was born in New York City in 1915. During World War II, he worked as a social psychologist exploring propaganda, public opinion and social attitudes for US Army intelligence. After obtaining his PhD at Harvard in 1947 he became a member of faculty, serving as professor of psychology, as well as co-founder and director of the Centre for Cognitive Studies.

Beginning in the 1940s, Bruner worked on the ways in which needs, motivations and expectations (or *mental sets*) influence perception. He explored perception from a functional orientation, as against a process to separate it from the world around it. In addition to this work, Bruner also began to consider the role of strategies in the process of human categorization, and more generally, the development of human cognition. This concern with cognitive psychology led to a particular interest in the cognitive development of children and their modes of representation. This led him naturally to consider what might be the appropriate forms of education.

From the late 1950s Bruner became more interested in schooling in the United States – and was invited to chair an influential ten-day meeting of scholars and educators at Woods Hole on Cape Cod in 1959, under the auspices of the National Academy of Sciences and the National Science Foundation. One result was Bruner's landmark book *The Process of Education* (1960). This book developed some of the key themes of that meeting and was a crucial factor in generating a range of educational programmes and experiments in the 1960s.

Bruner also became involved in the design and implementation of the influential *MAN: A Course of Study* (MACOS) project, which sought to produce a comprehensive curriculum drawing upon educational psychology. The organizing questions of MACOS are

- What makes human beings human?
- How did they get that way?
- How can they become more so?

Learners examine behaviour within a framework of cross-disciplinary and cross-cultural analysis to attain a more profound awareness of human nature and human culture. They develop a view of their own history and culture through multiple lenses. Several assumptions guided the design and development of the course:

- as learners increase their awareness of their own culture, they also experience an increased self-confidence and comprehension of their operating assumptions about life.
- learning is largely a social process by which learners and teachers articulate and share ideas with one another.

- the world can be observed, conjectured about, ordered and understood using the modes of inquiry of the biological and social sciences.
- an individual life can be viewed as part of the larger flow of human existence within a given environment.
- recurrent themes include the concepts of life cycle, learning, parental care, adaptation and selection, aggression, affection and love, social organization, language, technology and values and beliefs.

These themes are repeatedly examined from different perspectives throughout the course.

Instructional materials fall into **three** categories: 1) film and other visual aids; 2) written materials; and 3)interactive devices, such as games. Film, the primary source of data in the course, is used to simulate field observations. Thirty booklets of differing styles and purposes replace the usual textbook. In addition, field notes, journals, poems, songs and stories, games, construction exercises and observation projects allow children to learn in varied ways.

MACOS has been challenged, not least because of the cross-cultural nature of the materials. It was also said to be difficult to implement – requiring a high degree of sophistication and learning on the part of teachers, and ability and motivation on the part of learners. Some traditionalists were opposed ideologically to liberal and progressive thinking.

In the 1960s Bruner developed a theory of cognitive growth. His approach – in contrast to that of Piaget – examined environmental and experiential factors. Bruner suggested that intellectual ability developed in stages through step-by-step changes depending on how the mind is used. Bruner's thinking became increasingly influenced by writers like Lev Vygotsky and he began to be critical of the intrapersonal focus he had taken, and the lack of attention paid to social and political context. In the early 1970s Bruner left Harvard to teach for several years at the University of Oxford. There he continued his research into infant development and also began a series of explorations of the language of children.

Bruner by this time was becoming more critical of the 'cognitive revolution' and began to argue for the building of a cultural psychology. This interest was the subject matter of *The Culture of Education* (1996).

> It is surely the case that schooling is only one small part of how a culture inducts the young into its canonical ways. Indeed, schooling may even be at odds with a culture's other ways of inducting the young into the requirements of communal living . . .. What has become increasingly clear . . . is that education is not just about conventional school matters like curriculum or standards or testing. What we resolve to do in school only makes sense when considered in the broader context of what the society intends to accomplish through its educational investment in the young. How one conceives of education, we have finally come to recognize, is a function of how one conceives of culture and its aims, professed and otherwise. (Jerome S. Bruner 1996: ix–x)

Four key themes emerge:

1. The role of structure in learning and how it may be made central in teaching.

The approach taken should be a practical one. 'The teaching and learning of structure, rather than simply the mastery of facts and techniques, is at the centre of the classic problem of transfer . . . If earlier learning is to render later learning easier, it must do so by providing a general picture in terms of which the relations between things encountered earlier and later are made as clear as possible'

2. Readiness for learning.

Here the argument is that schools have wasted a great deal of time by postponing the teaching of important areas because they are perceived to be 'too difficult'.

Bruner begins with the hypothesis that any subject can be taught effectively in some intellectually honest form to any child at any stage of development. This notion underpins the idea of the *spiral curriculum* – 'A curriculum as it develops should revisit basic ideas repeatedly, building upon them until the learner has grasped the full formal apparatus that goes with them'

3. Intuitive and analytical thinking.

Intuition ('the intellectual technique of arriving at plausible but tentative formulations without going through the analytical steps by which such formulations would be found to be valid or invalid conclusions') is a much neglected but essential feature of productive thinking. Here Bruner notes how experts in different fields appear 'to leap intuitively into a decision or a solution to a problem' – a phenomenon that Donald Schön was to explore later in *Beyond the Stable State* (1973). Bruner also considers how teachers and schools might create the conditions for intuition to flourish.

4. Motives for learning.

'Ideally', Bruner writes, 'interest in the material to be learned is the best stimulus to learning, rather than such external goals as grades or later competitive advantage'. In an age of increasing spectatorship, 'motives for learning must be kept from going passive . . . they must be based as much as possible upon the arousal of interest in what there is be learned, and they must be kept broad and diverse in expression'.

Bruner wrote two postscripts to *The Process of Education*. These are: *Towards a Theory of Instruction* (1966) and *The Relevance of Education* (1971). In these books he puts forward his evolving ideas about the ways in which instruction actually affects the mental models of the world that learners construct, elaborate on and transform. In the first book the various essays deal with matters such as patterns of growth, the will to learn and on making and judging (including some helpful material on evaluation). Two essays are of particular interest – his reflections on MACOS and his 'notes on a theory of instruction'. The latter essay makes the case for taking into account questions of predisposition, structure, sequence and reinforcement in preparing curricula and programmes. He makes the case for education as a knowledge-getting process:

To instruct someone . . . is not a matter of getting him to commit results to mind. Rather, it is to teach him to participate in the process that makes possible the establishment of knowledge. We teach a subject not to produce little living libraries on that subject, but rather to get a learner to think mathematically for himself, to consider matters as an historian does, to take part in the process of knowledge-getting. Knowing is a process not a product. (1966: 72)

Bruner has had a profound effect on education – and upon those researchers and learners with whom he has worked. It is important that he suggests that a learner (even of a very young age) is capable of learning any material so long as the instruction is organized appropriately. This contrasts sharply with the beliefs of Piaget and other stage theorists.

Bruner's ideas are based on categorization. 'To perceive is to categorize, to conceptualize is to categorize, to learn is to form categories, to make decisions is to categorize.' People interpret the world in terms of its similarities and differences. Like Bloom's *Taxonomy*, Bruner suggests a system of coding in which people form a hierarchical arrangement of related categories. Each successively higher level of category becomes more specific, echoing Bloom's understanding of knowledge acquisition as well as the related idea of instructional scaffolding.

David Ausubel

Ausubel's first interest was medicine. He worked as an assistant surgeon and psychiatric resident with the US Public Health Service and immediately after World War II he worked in Germany in the medical treatment of displaced persons. After completing his training in psychiatry, Ausubel entered Columbia University and earned a doctorate in developmental psychology.

In 1950 he accepted a position with the Bureau of Educational Research at the University of Illinois. He remained with the Bureau for the next 16 years. In those years, he published extensively on cognitive psychology. He left the University of Illinois in 1966 in order to accept a position with the Department of Applied Psychology, Ontario Institute of Studies in Education. He was in Toronto for two years, 1966–8. He then moved to become Professor and Head of the Department of Educational Psychology at the University of New York, where he served until his retirement in 1975.

The overarching idea in Ausubel's theory is that knowledge is hierarchically organized; new information is meaningful to the extent that it can be related (attached, anchored) to what is already known. He stresses meaningful learning, as opposed to rote learning or memorization; and reception, or received knowledge, rather than discovery learning. Ausubel did not claim that discovery learning does not work; but that it is not efficient. For learning to be efficient, the learner has to see meanings in what is being learned.

Ausubel's theories have a number of teaching implications.

The advance organizer.

This may prove to be the most enduring of his ideas, even though it can often be difficult to implement. Learners need to be able to see the whole picture before details are learned. Without this large view, learners cannot make sense of details. Organization precedes detailed learning.

The comparative organizer.

How do we remember concepts and keep them from fading, or being lost in higher-level ideas? Ausubel proposed the comparative organizer as a way of enhancing the discrimination of ideas. Comparative organization allows a learner to recognize the similarities and differences in a set of related ideas.

Progressive differentiation.

According to Ausubel, the purpose of progressive differentiation is to increase the stability and clarity of anchoring ideas. The basic notion here is that in learning several related topics, success is more likely if the big ideas are dealt with first, and then later details can be elaborated.

In 1959, in *Viewpoints from Related Disciplines: Human Growth and Development,* Ausubel considered from the standpoint of developmental psychology the following issues:

- readiness as a criterion for curricular placement;
- developmental factors affecting breadth of the curriculum;
- the learner's voice in determining the curriculum;
- the content and goals of instruction in relation to the organization and growth of the intellect.

The learner's acquisition of a clear, stable, and organized body of knowledge . . . is the most significant independent variable influencing the learner's capacity for acquiring more new knowledge in the same field.

What works in classrooms, not in laboratory studies merely was the focus Ausubel preferred for educational psychology. His research rested on the premise that new learning takes place most effectively when it fits into schemes that already exist in a learner's mind. His advocacy of reception learning and expository teaching brought the

expression *advance organizers* into the common vocabulary and
practice of classroom teachers. We can think of the advance organizer as simply a device or a mental learning aid to help us 'get a grip'
on the new information. It is a means of preparing the learner's cognitive structure for the learning experience about to take place. It is
a device to activate the relevant schema or conceptual patterns so
that new information may be more readily subsumed into the learner's existing cognitive structure or mental depiction.

Ausubel's writings have not attracted the popularity of Bruner's
works. However, because much of his theory has been developed
from research in mainstream cognitive psychology, many of his
ideas have survived as part of information processing theory.

Robert Gagné

Gagné was an American. During and after World War 11 he developed instructional materials for air force pilot training. Later he
went on to develop a series of studies and works that helped codify
what is now considered to be 'good instruction.' He was also
involved in applying concepts of instructional theory to the design
of computer based training and multimedia based learning.

'Learning,' Gagne stated, 'is something that takes place inside a
person's head – in the brain.' This mentalist approach places him
firmly within the cognitive paradigm.

A major contribution to the theory of learning was the model
Nine Events of Instruction. These are

1. gain attention;
2. inform the learner of objectives;
3. stimulate recall of prior learning;
4. present stimulus material;
5. provide learner guidance;
6. elicit performance;
7. provide feedback;
8. assess performance;
9. enhance retention transfer.

Gagné's work is sometimes summarized as the Gagné Assumption. The assumption is that different types of learning exist, and

that varied instructional conditions are most likely to bring about these different types of learning.

Gagné identifies five major categories of learning:

1. verbal information;
2. intellectual skills;
3. cognitive strategies;
4. motor skills;
5. attitudes.

Different internal and external conditions are necessary for each type of learning. For example, for cognitive strategies to be learned, there must be a chance to practise the development of new solutions to problems; to learn attitudes, the learner must be exposed to a credible role model or to persuasive arguments.

Learning tasks for intellectual skills can be organized in a hierarchy according to complexity. The primary significance of the hierarchy is to identify prerequisites that should be completed to facilitate learning at each level. Prerequisites are identified by doing an analysis of a learning task. The importance for teaching is that learning hierarchies provide a basis for the sequencing of instruction. Much of what Gagné proposed has been incorporated into learning at many levels.

Albert Bandura

Bandura is a Canadian who has mostly worked in the United States. He directed his initial research to the role of social modelling in human motivation, thought and action. He engaged in studies of social learning and aggression. *Adolescent Aggression* was published in 1959, and *Aggression: A Social Learning Analysis* in 1973. His central concern was social learning theory and to the role that self-efficacy beliefs play in human functioning.

In 1986 Bandura published *Social Foundations of Thought and Action: A Social Cognitive Theory*, in which he offered a social cognitive theory of human functioning that accords a central role to cognitive, vicarious, self-regulatory and self-reflective processes in human adaptation and change. In this theory Bandura views people as

- self-organizing;
- proactive;

- self-reflecting;
- self-regulating.

Learners are not merely reactive organisms shaped by environmental forces or driven by inner impulses. Bandura's theory of self-efficacy can, he states, be applied to fields as apparently diverse as life-course development, education, health, psychopathology, athletics, business and international affairs. One area of particular interest for many people is how individuals use psycho-social tactics selectively in order to disengage moral self-sanctions from inhumane conduct. He has called for a civilized life with humane standards buttressed 'by safeguards built into social systems that uphold compassionate behaviour and renounce cruelty.'

Self-efficacy

By the mid-1980s Bandura had developed a social cognitive theory of human functioning. This theory accords a central role to cognitive, vicarious, self-regulatory and self-reflective processes in human adaptation and change. Human lives cannot be lived in isolation. People have shared beliefs about their capabilities and common aspirations to better their lives. In his 1997 book, *Self-Efficacy: The Exercise of Control*, Bandura sets out at considerable length the basic tenets of his theory of self-efficacy and its applications in many fields.

Human functioning is the product of a dynamic interplay of personal, behavioural and environmental influences. Bandura and others had not simply moved educational psychology far from behaviourism but also from social learning to social cognitive learning. By drawing on their symbolic capabilities, people can

- better understand their environment;
- construct guides for action;
- solve problems cognitively;
- support certain courses of action;
- gain new knowledge by reflective thought;
- communicate with others at any distance in time and space.

By symbolizing their experiences, people give structure, meaning and continuity to their lives. They develop the capacity for self-directedness and forethought. People plan courses of action, anticipate their likely consequences and set goals and challenges for themselves to motivate, guide and regulate their activities. After adopting personal standards, people regulate their own motivation and behaviour by the positive and negative consequences they produce for themselves. They do things that give them satisfaction and a sense of self-worth, and try to refrain from actions that evoke self-devaluing reactions. The human capacity for self-management is an aspect of the theory that makes it particularly apt to the changing times, with the accelerated pace of informational, social and technological changes. These points are important for teachers considering plans for motivation of learners.

The capability for self-reflection concerning one's functioning and personal efficacy is another human attribute that features prominently in social cognitive theory. Bandura regards the self-efficacy belief system as the foundation of human motivation, well-being and personal accomplishments. Unless people believe that they can bring about desired outcomes by their actions they have little incentive to act, or to persevere in the face of difficulties. A wealth of empirical evidence suggests that beliefs of personal efficacy touch virtually every aspect of people's lives – whether they think productively, self-debilitatingly, pessimistically or optimistically; how well they motivate themselves and persevere in the face of adversities; their vulnerability to stress and depression, and the life choices they make.

The reciprocal nature of the determinants of human functioning in social cognitive theory makes it possible for therapeutic and counselling efforts to be directed at personal, environmental or behavioural factors. Strategies for increasing well-being can be aimed at improving emotional, cognitive or motivational processes, thus increasing behavioural competencies, or changing the social conditions under which people live and work.

In school, for example, teachers have the challenge of improving the academic learning and confidence of learners. Using social cognitive theory as a framework, teachers can attempt to

- improve emotional states;
- correct faulty self-beliefs and habits of thinking (personal factors);
- improve academic skills and self-regulatory practices (behaviour);

- alter the school and classroom structures that may work to undermine success (environmental factors).

Social cognitive theory is founded on the view that individuals are agents proactively engaged in their own development and can make things happen by their actions.

Environments and social systems influence human behaviour through psychological mechanisms of the self system. Hence, social factors such as economic conditions, socio-economic status and educational and family structures do not directly affect human behaviour. Rather, they affect it to the degree that they influence people's aspirations, self-efficacy beliefs, personal standards, emotional states and other self-regulatory influences. In all, this social cognitive view of human and collective functioning – which marked a departure from the prevalent behaviourist and learning theories of the day – was to have a profound influence on psychological thinking and theorizing during the last two decades of the 20th century and into the new century.

As teachers know very well, individuals are typically guided by their beliefs when they engage the world, and those beliefs and reality are seldom perfectly matched. As a consequence, people's accomplishments are generally better predicted by their self-efficacy beliefs than by their previous attainments, knowledge or skills. Of course, no amount of confidence or self-appreciation can produce success when requisite skills and knowledge are absent. Typically, of course, self-efficacy beliefs help determine the outcomes one expects. Confident individuals anticipate successful outcomes; learners confident in their social skills anticipate successful social encounters. Those confident in their academic skills expect high marks in tests and examinations; they expect the quality of their work to reap personal and professional benefits. The opposite is true of those who lack confidence. Learners who doubt their social skills often envision rejection even before they establish social contact. Those who lack confidence in their academic skills envision low grades before they even enrol on a course, and thus unwittingly contribute to low grades and eventual failure.

Because individuals operate collectively as well as individually, self-efficacy is both a personal and a social construct. Collective systems develop a sense of collective efficacy, a group's shared belief in its capability to attain goals and accomplish desired tasks. For example, schools develop collective beliefs about the capability of their learners to learn, of their teachers to teach and otherwise enhance the lives of their learners, and of their administrators and policymakers to create environments conducive to these tasks. Organizations with a strong sense of collective efficacy exercise empowering influences on their constituent parts, and these effects are soon made evident.

It cannot be over-emphasized that, when exploring the relationship between efficacy and behaviour, we must be certain to measure the self-efficacy beliefs relevant to the behaviour in question, and vice versa. Faulty assessment of self or performance will create an ambiguous relationship. Bandura has argued that 'measures of self-precept must be tailored to the domain of psychological functioning being explored'. It is important to know the precise nature of the skills required to successfully perform a particular behaviour. Clearly, it is not simply a matter of how capable an individual is, but of how capable they believe they are.

Abraham Maslow

Maslow was an American psychologist. He is mostly noted today for his proposal of a hierarchy of human needs. He was not an educational psychologist: his lifelong research and thinking was about mental health and human potential. His conclusions have, however, affected thinking in several fields. Maslow's work is well known and has been influential.

In 1943 Maslow first wrote about the hierarchy of needs. Human needs are arranged like a ladder, a hierarchy. The most basic needs – those at the foot of the ladder – are physical needs: air, water, food, sex. Then come safety needs: security, stability; to be followed by psychological or social needs: belonging, love, acceptance. At the top of the ladder are self-actualizing needs: the need to fulfil oneself, to become all that one is capable of becoming.

Maslow felt that unfulfilled needs lower on the ladder would inhibit the person from climbing to the next step. People who successfully managed the highest level were what he called self-actualizing people.

Though familiar now, at the time Maslow's thinking was original. Most psychology before him had been concerned with the abnormal and the ill. He wanted to know what constituted positive mental health.

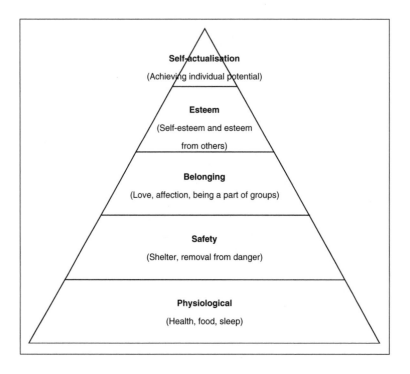

There are important applications for teachers seeking to motivate learners. We have to

- encourage learners to seek need fulfilment at the present level. To distract them from higher needs, threaten their lower needs.
- assist learners to meet the needs on which they are currently focused. Their attention is here and they will thank you for assistance in meeting their present needs.
- encourage them reach up to higher needs. Let them see and reach up to the greater things in life.
- create tensions which we can use for our own purposes in assisting learners.

Factors that demotivate

Frederick Herzberg, clinical psychologist and pioneer of 'job enrichment', is regarded as one of the great original thinkers in management and motivational theory. His book *The Motivation to Work*, written in 1959, first established his theories about motivation in the workplace. Herzberg's survey work, originally on 200 Pittsburgh engineers and accountants, remains a fundamentally important reference in motivational study. Conclusions were developed as the Two Factor Theory (also known as Herzberg's Motivation-Hygiene Theory) and states that there are certain factors in the workplace that cause job satisfaction, while a separate set of factors cause dissatisfaction. They are not simply opposing reactions to the same factors, as had always previously been believed.

Herzberg expanded his Motivation-Hygiene Theory in his subsequent books: *Work and the Nature of Man* (1966); *The Managerial Choice* (1982); and *Herzberg on Motivation* (1983). Significantly, Herzberg commented in 1984, 25 years after his theory was first published:

The original study has produced more replications than any other research in the history of industrial and organizational psychology

There are *motivators* which reinforce and produce satisfaction.

Other factors, which he called *hygiene factors,* lead to dissatisfaction.

Human beings have two sets of needs: as an animal to avoid pain; and as a human being to grow psychologically. Herzberg's ideas relate strongly to modern notions of ethical management and social responsibility. His ideas are just as relevant now as when he first suggested them, except that the implications of responsibility, fairness, justice and compassion in business are now global. As education develops managerial structures, Herzberg becomes more relevant in this sphere of activity also. It has to be stated that the theories were not developed in order to motivate and thus achieve better performance. They sought instead, primarily, to explain how to manage people properly, for the good of all people at work.

Herzberg's research proved that people will strive to achieve 'hygiene' needs because they are unhappy without them, but once satisfied the effect soon wears off – satisfaction is temporary. Then as now, poorly managed organizations fail to understand that people are not 'motivated' by addressing 'hygiene' needs. People are only truly motivated by enabling them to reach for and satisfy the factors that Herzberg identified as real motivators, such as personal growth, development, etc., which represent a far deeper level of meaning and fulfilment.

Examples of Herzberg's 'hygiene' needs (or maintenance factors) in the workplace are

- policy
- relationship with supervisor
- work conditions
- salary
- company car
- status
- security
- relationship with subordinates
- personal life

This research identified that true motivators were other completely different factors, notably

- achievement
- recognition
- the nature of the work itself
- levels of responsibility
- opportunities for advancement
- opportunities for personal growth

The absence of any serious challenge to Herzberg's theory continues effectively to validate it.

Conclusions

In not much more than a hundred years, educational psychology has undergone many changes. Perhaps the most significant change is that research which was almost entirely concerned with teaching is now learner-oriented. The two processes, teaching and learning, are of course inextricably linked, but the shift of emphasis has been real and it has been important.

There are a number of conclusions that teachers can draw, both from their reading and from their everyday experiences in the real world. These everyday experiences are important. Education takes place in many places, as well as classrooms, and not in the psychologist's study or the research laboratory. No amount of theory will compensate a teacher faced by a group of youngsters destroying classroom furniture and offering verbal and physical violence.

Research has generally shown that for learners to maintain motivation they need to be able to

- have the belief that they possess the skills and competencies to successfully accomplish their learning goals.
- see relevance to their learning;
- be responsible agents in the definition and accomplishment of personal goals.
- understand the higher level thinking and self-regulation skills that lead to goal attainment.
- control emotions and moods that facilitate or interfere with learning and motivation.
- understand the processes for effectively and efficiently encoding, processing and retrieving information.
- produce performance outcomes that signal successful goal attainment.

Teachers need to be involved in facilitating these learner processes and outcomes. This means you must know the learners well in order to motivate them to produce their best possible work. Getting to know learners does not mean joining in their social activities. Going down to the local pub with older learners can seriously affect a teacher's pocket.

There is no better way, perhaps, of achieving the conditions for motivation than personal contact with learners. Meet learners regularly in order to get to know them personally. The best way is by meeting small groups or pairs of learners in your office at different times. Alas, it is not wise to meet learners alone, particularly members of the opposite sex. Exemplary teachers have found themselves accused of many things.

You may wish to invite learners to complete a questionnaire on their personal and educational backgrounds, their hopes and aspirations. Completion should be entirely voluntary. The answers could form the basis of the first discussion period out of class hours.

When you mark and evaluate work, be sure it is thorough and honest. Praise of poor work or attitudes never has positive outcomes, no matter how well meaning such praise may be. That said, it is always possible to find a positive comment you can make. Suggestions on how to improve performance may appear to be unwelcome but will pay dividends in the long run.

Many learners enter a course of study enthusiastic about learning, but need and expect their teachers to inspire, stimulate and challenge them. The effective teacher takes that initial enthusiasm and harnesses it. This is motivation.

Remember

- to help learners feel that they are valued members of a learning community;
- to maintain interest, while accepting that every period of learning cannot be one of high enthusiasm. Keep the learners' eyes fixed on the ultimate goals.
- to assist learners in finding personal meaning and value in the learning and assignments;
- to create an atmosphere that is open and positive, while still maintaining levels of discipline acceptable to you and the institution in which you work;
- to give frequent, early, positive feedback that supports learners' beliefs that they can do well. Work handed in and then ignored for weeks is a certain way to demotivate learners.
- to ensure opportunities for learners' success by assigning tasks that are neither too easy nor too difficult.

What happens if you personally find the material boring? After all, there is surely a limit to the number of years you can teach even a wonderful play like *Macbeth* to a grade 11 class. The answer is that you have to grit your teeth, smile and behave as if this is not only the greatest play in the world, but one that you enjoy above all others. You have to fake sincerity, and, as someone once said, if you can fake that you have it made.

It is also true, and there is ample research to support this assertion, that good everyday teaching practices do more to counter learner apathy than special efforts by you or the department to attack apathy directly. Most learners respond positively to a well-organized course taught by an enthusiastic teacher who has a genuine interest in the subject matter, in learners as individuals, and what they learn and the promotion of successful outcomes. Thus activities you undertake to promote learning will also enhance learners' motivation.

Capitalize on learners' existing needs. Learners learn best when incentives for learning satisfy their own motives. Some of the needs your learners may bring to the class are

- the need to learn something in order to complete a particular task;
- the need to seek new experiences;
- the need to perfect skills;
- the need to overcome challenges;
- the need to become competent;
- the need to succeed and do well, not least in external examinations;
- the need to be part of a group and to interact with other people.

These are essentially all the same but different learners couch them in different terms.

Satisfying such needs is rewarding in itself, and such rewards sustain learning more effectively than do high marks or grades. The responsibility of the teacher who wishes to motivate successfully – and that surely means all teachers, no matter what they say in the staff common room – is to design activities, assignments and discussion questions to address the needs.

Allow learners to be active participants in learning. Learners learn in a variety of ways:

- by doing;
- designing;
- creating;
- making;
- solving problems;
- taking tests;
- making presentations;
- writing reports.

Passivity dampens learners' curiosity. In the making of movies there is a good piece of advice for directors: Don't tell, show! The same with teaching and learning: Don't tell, ask! Encourage learners to suggest approaches to a problem or to guess the results of an experiment. Use small group work or work in pairs. (There is more about such strategies in the third section of this book.)

Have high expectations of your learners and let them know what your expectations are. Be sure the expectations are realistic, however. A teacher's expectations have a powerful effect on a learner's performance. If you act as though you expect your learners to be motivated, hardworking and interested in the course, they are more likely to be so. Set realistic expectations for learners when you make assignments, give presentations, conduct discussions and grade examinations. Realistic enough to motivate learners to do their best work but not so high that they are inevitably going to be frustrated in trying to meet impossible demands. Provide opportunities for learners to experience success. Some of them may have been acquainted with failure all their lives.

Invite the learners to analyze what makes classes more or less successful. (You may prefer to avoid reference to motivation.) Ask learners to compare two recent sessions, one that was successful and interesting, and one they found less successful, even boring. Allow the learners to work in small groups or in pairs. Invite them to discuss and write down the points that they believe led to success or otherwise. You may discover that each group or pair will reach roughly the same conclusions.

- Organization of the class.
- Relevance of the material being learned.
- Difficulty level of the material
- Opportunities for active involvement.
- Variety of tasks proposed.
- Rapport between teacher and learners

Strengthening learners' self-motivation is vitally important.

Avoid
- Avoid language that emphasizes your position as a teacher. At the same time do not try to be one of the gang.

- Avoid the contemporary slang used by young learners. They will not like you better, and it may even alienate them.
- Intense competition, which may create unnecessary tensions and stop losers from learning successfully.
- Public criticism of individuals. You may wish to criticize adversely but do this privately on a one-to-one basis.
- Too much individual work. Cooperation, especially in primary schools and the early years of the secondary phase, produces the best results.
- Listening to gossip, as this suggests you are taking sides.
- Showing that you find the tasks and the material boring, even if you are suffering from burn-out in some respects.

Motivation does not last forever. The teacher needs to devise ways of motivating learners on a regular basis. Where there are rewards, these need to be varied. Rewards can be given to individuals or to groups. The withdrawal of recognition or rewards can also have a motivating effect.

Points for discussion
Finally, we offer the following conclusions for discussion or for private thought.

Research on academic achievement motivation has increasingly focused on learners' goals. Most of that research has focused on two particular types of achievement objectives: task goals and ability goals. Examination of social goals can lead to a better understanding of motivation and achievement in schools. Social goals, social influences, have an important impact on attitudes to learning. Teachers and managers need to give more consideration to the ways in which the learning environment may influence learners' social goal orientations and their behaviour.

Most people want to have, or to achieve in the future, a large measure of control over their lives. They want to feel that their actions will make a difference. Few people wish to believe that they are mere creatures of circumstance, subjected to a blind destiny. Thus, there remains a general belief in free will as opposed to necessity. What we do, therefore, is within our own levels of competence.

If teachers want to motivate learners, they must themselves be motivated, and let it show. Clear goals should be devised and the information passed on to learners. Without teacher motivation there is likely to be hostility from the learners.

All learning, not least Competence Based Education and Training (CBET) has to allow learners a large measure of control over learning and predicted outcomes. This may lead to independent learning and self-motivation.

There should be some form of recognition for all learners. Recognition implies reward. While we do not advocate that all should receive a medal, for all are clearly not heroes, nevertheless there has to be a reward of some kind. It may be a certificate relating to effort. Or perhaps simply a word of approval in front of the whole group. Group recognition is often very important to learners.

It is unrealistic to expect an individual or group to be motivated in every situation. A learner may be highly motivated on the football field but show no interest during English lessons. Similarly, an interest in literature in English may not be duplicated in science classes.

Where learners participate in the setting of objectives and processes, they are more likely to be motivated for longer periods.

A teacher should strive in all ethical ways to have learners embrace goals agreed by the whole group. Where learners are part of a successful group – or part of a group still striving for success – they are more likely to be motivated than if pursuing individual goals. There are exceptions to this, however. Some learners actually prefer individual effort. Teachers must ensure that there is a place for the chess player as well as the team player.

Evidence of progress is a motivating factor. Success, no matter how small or how transient, motivates. Opportunities for success must be realistic. It is foolish to reward poor outcomes simply in order to provide a false notion of progress, or to provide an opportunity for praise.

Planning for motivation success is very important to the teacher. It is as important as planning a lesson or a teaching strategy.

We have presented the theories and the activities as we – practising teachers for many years – understand them. Unfortunately, there is no single magical formula for motivating learners.

It will be clear by now that many factors affect a learner's motivation. These include

- interest in the subject matter;
- perceptions of its usefulness to learning or to life;
- a general desire to achieve self-confidence and self-esteem;
- an individual's ability to work successfully within a group;
- levels of patience and persistence.

And, of course, not all learners are motivated by the same values, needs, desires or wants. Some of your learners will be motivated by the approval of others, some by overcoming challenges. Therefore, strive to know members of the class or course as individuals.

We have kept the description of theories to a minimum, the level needed to understand them. Fuller treatments can be found elsewhere. Our purpose has been to present the theories in outline and then relate them to practical suggestions for teachers, not least those new to the teaching profession. You may wish to apply these practical suggestions to planning your teaching methods, which, conveniently, is the matter of section three.

3   Planning teaching methods

Questions begin in childhood and parents all know how persistent such questions can be. Most of them begin with a WH word: Where, Who, What, When, Which. And as the child grows and develops, there is a need to answer many questions too, whether in a learning situation, a job interview, a police station, when meeting someone who interests us more than ordinarily, or whatever situation we find ourselves in. It is said of Gertrude Stein, American author, that as she lay dying she asked her partner, *What is the answer?* and on receiving no response, asked, *In that case, what is the question?* This is perhaps more profound than at first appears to be the case.

Asking questions is the heart of all learning. Quite literally, everything begins with questions. There is a collection of related techniques, known as *learning methods*, that have been developed over the years. However, before the methods or the theories, there came the questions. That said, it is incumbent on us to present as objectively as possible different teaching methods and how to plan for their most effective use. All involve questioning of some kind, whether in oral or written form, and some questions might remain formed or unspoken and exercise only our inner selves.

Lectures

The lecture in its many forms remains a commonly used method for transferring information to large groups. The method has long been used, having been established formally centuries ago as a teaching process that began with a reading of important passages from the text by the master, followed by his interpretation of the text. Learners were expected to sit, listen, say nothing and make notes.

There are, as there always have been, serious questions regarding the effectiveness of this traditional lecture approach. One criticism has been that people delivering lectures have usually not received proper training in how best and most effectively to deliver a lecture. Many university lecturers often read, in varying degrees of audibility, the latest chapter from their forthcoming book or piece of research, and then left the rostrum without even taking questions. Others – A. J. P. Taylor the historian was an example – delivered interesting lectures, in Taylor's case without notes.

Many would now agree that the lecture method, where information is transferred from one brain to several others, with no intervening active processes, is outdated and ineffective. Successful learning is active learning. The lecture method is condemned as ineffective because it is passive, a one-way process that lacks discussion and is not accompanied by immediate practice and reinforcement. Any discussion of the material, and any subsequent questioning – and this was true in the older universities – took place in tutorials, which could be individual or in small groups, and could take place several days after the delivery of the lecture. It was little wonder that learners in universities preferred to skip lectures and to read from textbooks.

Despite these criticisms, which centre on the lack of interaction between teacher and learner, there is still a case to be made for using the lecture method, which can prove effective when allied with other teaching methods. As with any teaching method, whether or not it is effective or ineffective, lecturing depends to a large extent on the teacher. To condemn the lecture method out of hand because it is not interactive, because the teacher stands at a lectern and drones on in an uninteresting way, is about as useful as condemning interactive teaching methods because the teacher is always tired and clearly not interested in teaching. What is true, however, is that lecturers have usually wrongly estimated the length of time that learners can concentrate and remain engaged, and with serious consequences.

What constitutes an ineffective lecture?
- Too much talk by the teacher;
- Passive, one-way communication;

- No chance to ask questions in order to make a difficult point clearer;
- Only one source of information or opinion;
- Note taking without understanding is required;
- Lack of supporting media;
- Lack of activity by learners.

Delivery of a lecture
Delivering a successful lecture is possible, and sometimes desirable. It need not be simply a matter of standing in front of a class and reciting what you know. A lecture is a special form of communication in which voice, gesture, movement, facial expression and eye contact either complement or detract from the content. No matter what your topic, your delivery and manner of speaking influence learners' attentiveness and subsequent success in learning.

We suggest, therefore

- That you learn best practice by attending the lectures of other teachers;
- Watch yourself on videotape. Note and eradicate any features that will lead to learner inattentiveness;
- Choose a stance that is neither too formal nor too informal. Do not stand in such a way that indicates you want to be one of the gang. Learners are never fooled by this.
- Maintain eye contact as often as possible;
- Keep your tone of voice conversational.
- Speak with confidence.
- Do not merely recite from a written text. Allow the lecture to have some of the characteristics of a discussion, or even a conversation.
- Try not to show any nervousness you might feel. This can often be achieved by avoiding a cold start. Start with a joke, perhaps, but be careful to remember this is a lecture and not a stage routine. Ask a challenging question, perhaps. Mix with learners informally before you begin the lecture. However you do it, achieve initial *rapport* with the learners.
- Avoid using the same techniques on a regular basis. Remember that variety is the spice of teaching as it is of life itself.

- Be sure that the learners know the objectives of the lecture.
- During the lecture make sure you are audible. Either project your voice or use a microphone.
- Vary the rate at which you speak.
- Pitch, volume and the intensity of your voice can all be used to maintain interest in the matter of your lecture. Do not allow your voice to fall at the ends of sentences.
- Avoid expressions which appear to suggest hesitation and lack of knowledge. These include: er, um, now where were we?
- Avoid long silences.
- Do not be afraid of admitting, if you allow questions or interruptions, that there is something of which you are ignorant.
- Keep a track of time but do not often look at your wrist watch. Put the watch on the table or lectern where it can be seen easily.
- In case you are running short of time, have a fall-back plan. Know in advance what can be omitted. Refer the learners to the notes that you will hand out.

Phasing a lecture
Phasing a lecture is very important.
An effective lecture presentation has three phases: Set, Body, Close. Or, if you prefer, as we do, *beginning, middle* and *end*.

Beginning
- Introduce the content
- Make clear the objectives
- Create initial interest

Middle
- Outline the major points of the lecture
- Recite in an interesting way the matter of the lecture
- Repeat points in different ways to establish the material
- Make connections with past learning

End
- Summarize the major points
- Distribute notes and any other handouts

- Mention any follow-up tutorials or similar meetings
- Introduce briefly the material of the next lecture in the series

We have shown that lecturing can be adversely criticized on pedagogical grounds but can also be a useful teaching technique if a number of suggestions are followed. The lecture method remains the best option for transmitting information and opinions simultaneously to large groups of people. In this way it is an economical tool for learning.

It is not useful to contrast the lecture method to active learning. All forms of learning can be made active. How the lecture is structured and delivered is the main point that relates to its success as a teaching tool. For cheapness, the lecture method can hardly be bettered. If nothing else, this appeals to managers who always complain of financial stringency.

Delivered by talented practitioners, lectures can be informative, controversial and exciting.

Demonstrations

The central point of teaching is to enable learners to understand better. What they need to understand is processes as well as factual material.

A demonstration is a very good way of teaching both practical skills and knowledge. The steps are simple: the teacher demonstrates something, and then the learner repeats the same demonstration or something similar.

Among the best places for demonstrations are

- a kitchen
- an office
- a garage
- a science laboratory
- a carpentry or a joiner's workshop
- a factory
- a hospital ward

It will be obvious from this list that demonstrations are suitable for showing and transmitting skills.

Reasons for using interactive demonstrations

Research and experience show that learners acquire significantly greater understanding of course material, especially the acquisition of a skill, when they observe and then repeat the skill. Demonstrations can be particularly successful when combined with lectures. Interactive demonstrations enable learners to be actively engaged. They also provide opportunities for critical thinking and reflection. A demonstration of a skill allows an opportunity for the learner to repeat a skill many times, until there is ease and facility in performing the skill.

When prepared carefully, and executed correctly, demonstrations can better illustrate important skills – allied to knowledge – than a conventional lecture. Learners are provoked to think and then allowed to do. This encourages independent thought.

Demonstrations are especially effective if

- they have a surprise effect;
- challenge an assumption;
- correct a misconception;
- illustrate an otherwise abstract concept or process.

Whatever the subject matter, demonstrations take place in real time. This can apply to a very wide range of skills. These can vary from demonstrating mouth-to-mouth resuscitation, through mending a bicycle puncture, to dealing with an experiment in physics, biology or chemistry.

Famous examples of science demonstrations include Michael Faraday's Christmas lectures for young people at the Royal Institution, inaugurated in 1826, and which have continued to the present day. Although billed as lectures, they would perhaps be better if known as demonstrations. Perhaps the most famous were the series of six delivered by Faraday in 1860 on *The Chemical History of the Candle*.

In preparing a demonstration the teacher needs to ask a number of pertinent questions. These include asking:

- What concepts do we want the demonstration to illustrate?
- Which demonstrations on the selected topic will generate the greatest enhancement in learner learning?

- What prior knowledge should be reviewed before the demonstration?
- When during the class would a demonstration be most effective?
- What steps in the demonstration procedure should be carried out ahead of time?
- What questions will be appropriate to direct learner observation and thought processes
  - before
  - during
  - after the demonstration?
- What follow-up questions can be used to enhance learners' understanding of the new concept or skill?

Demonstrations that use everyday objects require little preparation. For Faraday it was a candle; for T H Huxley, a piece of chalk. For demonstrations that will be repeated, all the items the teacher needs can be stored and retrieved and reassembled for subsequent demonstrations. As the demonstration progresses there can be a dialogue between the teacher and the observers. It is important, therefore, that classes are not too large. All learners should have an unimpeded view of whatever skill is being demonstrated. Without such a view, success in repeating the skill is likely to be limited and partial.

Demonstrations of lessons for teachers are important. The demonstration can be an example of best practice. Without these, teachers still learning will simply replicate what they remember from their own schooldays.

Demonstration lesson plan
Purpose

The purpose of this demonstration is to:

- provide learners with an opportunity to conduct a scientific demonstration to their peer group;
- assist learners in understanding the basic requirements for creating a lesson plan and how to ask relevant questions during a presentation;
- develop understanding of the scientific principles that are related to the demonstration.

You will use the Predict, Observe, Explain technique when delivering your demonstration. This technique will help you develop your questioning skills as well as engage your learners in the lesson.

Task

This demonstration consists of several parts. It is a 15 minute science demonstration to a small group of your peers. This demonstration will be videotaped.

- Learners are informed of the objectives of the demonstration.
- Questions are asked which are designed to stimulate thinking.
- Learners are asked to predict what will happen.
- They will observe the demonstration.

The learners may be an actual class or a group made up of peers.

Specimen peer evaluation form

Peer Evaluation of _____

Your Name: _____

Please provide an evaluation and constructive feedback on your colleague's Peer Teaching.

Ask yourself:

- Is the teacher well prepared?
- Does the teacher make good use of visual aids, models and other non-verbal representations?
- Is the presentation interesting and comprehensible?
- Is there effective communication?
- Does the teacher use humour and creativity?
- What are the effective parts of the demonstration?

Specimen lesson plan evaluation template

Demonstration addresses stated objectives	1	2	3	4	5
Description and rationale for prerequisites	1	2	3	4	5
Details and procedures of the demonstration	1	2	3	4	5
Effective questioning strategy	1	2	3	4	5
Explanation of the scientific principle	1	2	3	4	5
Use of handout material	1	2	3	4	5
Safety issues identified	1	2	3	4	5

Question and answer techniques

There are **two** main divisions within questions: oral and written. Within the two divisions, there are many sub-divisions.

Teaching is often not successful because learners are unable to answer the questions they are asked or teachers answer questions that learners have not asked. Using effective questioning techniques assists successful learning. Helping learners to ask good questions for themselves will help them to continue to learn. How do you help learners to move from answering your questions to asking good questions for themselves? A short answer would be: by paying explicit attention to the uses of questions and to the nature of successful questions.

Why do teachers ask questions?

- The questioner really wants something answered. The answer may be known, as in teaching, or unknown, as in someone genuinely seeking information.

    'Why did Oscar Wilde decide to live in France on his release from prison?'

    'Is this the way to Victoria station, please?'

- To discover what has been learned from an activity, from the lecture, from reading, from the learner's last assignment, or perhaps from the previous ten minutes of discussion.

    'Why do you think Shakespeare breaks up the dialogue between Macbeth and his wife in Act 2 sc ii?'

- To initiate a discussion – to prompt a debate, to help learners develop their analytic faculties.

    'What other approaches did the lecturer suggest to this question?'

- To provide appropriate additional input, to introduce a mini-presentation on something which is obviously causing problems for most of the group.

    'So how can we draw these conflicting views together?'

- Opens up a topic;

    'What happens when red blood cells reach the spleen?'

- Explicitly builds on current knowledge;

    'How can governments control inflation?'

- Provokes a response from learners;

'Do you agree that Hitler's policies were good for the country at that time?'
- Leads the learner through a chain of reasoning.
 'What should we do if the bleeding doesn't stop?'

It is palpably clear that these questions are not all of the same type or on the same level. Whether oral or written, teachers should structure questions according to levels. These are

- Factual questions;
- Inferential questions;
- Analytical questions;
- Evaluative Questions.

Different kinds of questions prompt different kinds of answers, and hence different kinds of learning. Quite often, perhaps without being fully aware of what they are doing, teachers ask questions at levels inappropriate for the learners (whether too difficult or too easy) or they provide answers themselves without allowing the learners time to frame their own answers. Teachers also learn not to answer certain questions directly, for a variety of reasons.

Teachers have to learn how much detail to provide in an answer, or whether to answer the question at all. A question asked in good faith, requires an answer of some kind. A sensible first step is to check that you have understood the question – a brilliant five-minute answer to the wrong question is a waste of valuable time 'So are you asking . . .?' is a useful start to such a checking question. Many people will remember the old story of a mother who was asked by a small child where he came from. The mother, sensing this was the time to put her advanced and liberal views on child-rearing into action, settles the child down and then gives a biological explanation of seeds and eggs coming together. After a long explanation, the mother says, 'And that is where you came from.' To which the child replies, 'That's funny, because Johnny next door comes from Sheffield.'

Once you have the question clear, try a short answer and then check whether this is sufficient for the questioner. It often is. If not, it makes sense to check with other members of the class, to discover if they too require an answer to this particular question. If an answer is required by only one learner, or perhaps two, it may be best answered at the end of the session, or quietly in a corner. As well as giving an answer, also tell the questioner where they can find more information.

We have all as youngsters met with the old trick of the teacher who did not know or did not care. The answer to a question was often, 'Let's all find out for homework, shall we?' Only one person finds the answer that evening, and that is the teacher.

Or consider another trick, or stratagem, that is more worthy and valuable. *'That is a really interesting question. What do you think? What do others think?'* Reflecting the question back to the questioner carries a number of messages. It suggests

- that questioning is an important part of learning, which it is;
- that learning can be a collaborative enterprise, which it often is;
- that learning is sometimes a matter of constructing and even negotiating meaning.

This third suggestion is proof enough, if proof were needed, that the old notion of learning as a process of receiving knowledge and wisdom from an *expert* has long been, like Bunbury, quite exploded. It may, of course, if resorted to too often, also suggest that you do not know the answer. If this is the case, say so. Admitting to not knowing also carries the message that it is acceptable to admit ignorance so long as you can offer a way to find out and thus remove it.

There are variations on the stratagem of reflecting the question back at the questioner. Vary your approach.

'Could you put that question in another way?'
'What would be for you a satisfactory answer to that particular question?'

Teachers can develop useful supplementary questions. These are all legitimate so long as the purpose is to assist learners to find ways of making progress. Your answers to questions will depend on the time and place, the levels of the learners, and the outcomes you expect of a teaching session.

Asking a question is an action; answering a question is an action; debating what makes a good question or an acceptable answer is also an action, and can be intellectually and personally challenging. Learning is an active process.

Here are three real-life examples of how teachers dealt with questions.

A teacher new to a school introduces herself to a class, giving her surname, and her status as Mrs, a married woman. One child immediately asks the teacher her first name. The teacher ignores the question, but does not upbraid the child. The register is taken and the question is never asked again.

A youth asks a teacher, in confidence and after a general studies class about gender within society, about the causes of homosexuality. The class is composed of boastful young motor vehicle mechanics with apparently high testosterone levels. The teacher recognizes that the learner, a quiet member of the class, not given to boasting, has private reasons for asking the question. So the teacher evades the question directly but promises to include it in a future discussion – and keeps the promise.

A teacher of English in Zambia is timetabled for biology with a matriculating class. The teacher's knowledge of anatomy and physiology is comprehensive but of botany is woefully weak. At the beginning of a session, intended for the conduct of a test, a learner asks the teacher what a *bract* is. The teacher, sensing that the question may not merely be an attempt to delay the start of the test, promises to answer the question when the test has been concluded, at the end of the session. The class settle down to take the written test. The teacher, after a decent interval, strolls into the adjoining stock room and finds out from a botany book what a *bract* is. Examples are to be found on bougainvillea and there is a bush growing just outside the classroom door. At the end of the session, the test taken and marked (to give immediate knowledge of results), the teacher announces that the class may leave. He pretends to have forgotten the question. The learner, confident the teacher does not know, reminds the teacher of the question. The teacher expresses surprise that at this stage in the course the questioner does not know what a bract is. The class assembles round the bougainvillea bush and all is made clear. Some plants have poor, small flowers that will not attract insects. So leaves develop those mimic petals.

An example is the bougainvillea, which explains why the colourful *petals* remain on the plant for such a large part of the year.

Those were examples of oral questions. Written questions are an altogether different proposition. Once again, however, we are dealing with different types of questions at different levels.

- Factual questions;
- Inferential questions;
- Analytical questions;
- Evaluative Questions.

For most teachers there will never be a request from a publisher to write a textbook. They should be thankful for this: the expenditure of time is great; and the financial rewards invariably poor. However, teachers are required to frame questions for tests and for examinations. Unless they shamelessly lift questions from textbooks – and this is not recommended, for not all textbooks are reliable – it is incumbent on teachers to know how and why to frame questions. Whether dealing with a factual text or something from fiction, whether the subject area is literature in English, a passage for comprehension, or subject matter taken from the sciences, history, geography, or whatever, the principles remain the same. Suit the questions to the age of the learner. Ensure there are different levels of questioning. Anyone who has had the arduous task of marking examination papers, will have discovered that learners often do well on the first level of questioning, but are often less confident thereafter. That is one of the purposes of choosing levels with care, so that learners are able to use different skills.

Interest
First and foremost, material must be of interest to the target learners. And deciding what is interesting to learners is not always easy. What we think will go over well, often falls flat. When we search for reasons, we may find them beyond the text for questioning, and within our own approach and teaching style. An external explanation may well be timetabling, of course: double mathematics on Friday afternoon will, we can safely say, generally have less appeal than double games.

Vocabulary

Vocabulary levels in questioning need to be appropriate for the age and abilities of learners. Words that are unfamiliar – and new stock should be introduced – can either be glossed within the text, or included in a short glossary. Be careful not to overload the text with new or difficult words. We have been asked to write passages for comprehension by adolescent learners of English as a foreign language. There were two stipulations: the passages must be about 400 words long, and there must be a glossary of at least ten items. We concluded this was overload, and said so, but the publisher insisted, and we obeyed. (It was not, let us hasten to add, the esteemed publisher of the present work.)

Too much concern with words and their meanings inhibits other important aspects of comprehension. If many words need glossing, then the passage is not suitable for the target learners.

Grammatical structures

These are as important as vocabulary, whether we are devising questions for first-language learners or ESL/EFL learners. If questions are carefully graded, then levels can be slightly above the present abilities of a learner. There has to be room for effort, in order to achieve progress. This is important in questioning. If the horizon does not keep receding, we cannot move forward.

Of course, care has to be taken not to be too dogmatic. An example from a teacher training college in southern Africa may illustrate this point. We had to go out and observe young aspirant teachers in classrooms. The first class was an English language lesson. A common error – if error it really was – in the language of the youngsters was the use of *succeeding to*, as in *I was succeeding to complete my assignment*. The teacher was in no doubt, corrected the error with several examples, and repeated the point relentlessly. At the end of the session, the learners were sure, and the teacher was satisfied. The class then trooped to a history lesson in another room. The teacher there opened the lesson with the information that: *In 1837 Princess Victoria succeeded to the throne.* There was uproar; the learners were having none of it. Perhaps mercifully, the rest of that lesson has long been forgotten.

Written questions relate to a body of interactions. Learners take several meanings from a printed page. The reader interacts with the writer of the questions. There are interactions with other learners too. Teachers must be prepared for the fact that learners will react in different ways. It must also be remembered that learners will accept or reject material according to criteria the teacher will not always share.

- Factual questions;
- Inferential questions;
- Analytical questions;
- Evaluative questions.

There is no need to apologize for giving this list again.

Factual questions

These may seem the easiest questions to frame, and they are, as long as care is taken to ensure that only *facts* are being questioned. Do not move beyond facts to ask what may be *implicit* within a text. Those implicit features can be questioned elsewhere and in different ways. In a textbook that is graded, the opening passages may only ask factual questions, while later on many question types will be included. Factual questions are asked in order to ensure that the learner understands the passage.

But be careful! We have seen many examples in textbooks, and many more in classrooms, of factual questions that can be answered without understanding. Here in an example we used some years ago to exemplify this point.

THE GOOLIGOG STROTHED UP THE STRUMPER.

Q   Who or what strothed up the strumper?
A   The gooligog.
Q   What did the gooligog do?
A   Strothed.
Q   Where did the golligog strothe?
A   Up the strumper.

3 marks out of 3. 100%. Well done, followed by a red tick.

This is a simple, and at first sight perhaps rather silly, example but it shows how often a learner can achieve good marks and yet fail to understand. Nor is it a matter of merely guessing. Some form of comprehension is occurring but it is not what the teacher intended or expected. And let us not forget: for many learners, and not only those using English as a second or foreign language, this is what words on a page can look like.

Inferential questions
These are questions that take the reader beyond the factual level. We usually say that they are inferential but a simpler way of putting this is to talk about *going deeper* or *reading between the lines*. We do this every day, when reading a newspaper, a novel or listening to the news on radio or television. In a passage of fiction, a learner can be asked to predict events, basing predictions on what they already know of a character and that character's actions and responses so far. A violent alcoholic, when coming up against a weak spouse, can be predicted to behave in a violent fashion. A tough hero taking instruction in how to use modern hand guns can be expected to use such a weapon in the tale's dénouement.

In addition, a reader always brings to a text, whether fiction or nonfiction, their own previous knowledge, and a set of predispositions, whether opinions already held, as well as beliefs and prejudices. Faced with a passage based on natural selection and evolution, some readers raised in various religious sects will immediately *switch off*.

Examples of reading between the lines, taken from a comprehension passage whose subject was Chinese cooking, included the following:

- Why is rice used a lot in Chinese cookery?
- Why are pork and chicken staple parts of Chinese cookery?
- Why is wine optional in some recipes?
- What is corn flour used for?
- Why are instructions presented in very simple English?

Analytical questions
Age is a factor in the ability to ask questions, and also in the ability to understand what a question is. Young children do not always

understand the purpose of responding to a question with another question. It is in such an area that Piaget's stages of development assume a measure of relevance. More recent studies have suggested that a teacher's questioning reply to a child's question does not produce increases in children's questioning behaviour. That admitted, even young children can deal with questions that refer to problem solving as long as the questions are couched in language levels appropriate for the age group.

After setting the stage with introductory (factual and inferential) questions, teachers can then move on to analytical questioning for further critical inquiry. By focusing on specific elements, it is possible to connect to more complex levels. In problem-solving there are no right or wrong ways to ask questions and no obviously correct answer. What solves a problem is correct.

Evaluative questions
Few textbooks at primary or secondary levels pay enough, if any, attention to evaluation. Learners are sometimes asked to complete a form giving responses to a text, especially fiction, with the name Library Report or something similar. Yet even here there is usually mere description of the plot and naming the characters than to evaluation of the text as a whole.

Teachers are implored not to neglect evaluation, even at primary level. It is a matter of asking the right questions in the right language. The questions can be written as:

'What do you think . . . .?'
'Which passage did you enjoy most?'
'Do you intend to look out for other books by this author?'

An appraisal sheet for a piece of fiction might take the following lines.

APPRAISAL SHEET

LEARNER'S NAME
TITLE OF STORY
AUTHOR
MAIN CHARACTER
OTHER MAIN CHARACTERS

MINOR CHARACTERS
THEMES

YOUR RESPONSE TO THE STORY

++	very good
+	good
-	poor
--	very poor

Place on the following scale: 1 is low; 10 is high
Place a circle round your choice: 1 2 3 4 5 6 7 8 9 10

To assist the learners with themes, you can make a list of possible themes to be found in their reading. This is easier if the reading is from a class library of sets that you or colleagues have chosen.

Themes
- Disputes, conflicts, arguments within families, between friends or within groups of people.
- Modern versus traditional.
- Society and individuals. A person and how they relate to a group. The group can be a club, a class at school, a village or even a whole nation.
- The place of women and children in the modern world.
- The environment. How individuals or groups react to and with the events of global warming, weather changes, monsoons and flooding and care of animals.
- Violence and death and how they affect individuals or groups.
- Moral choices. Choosing what is right or wrong, acceptable or unacceptable behaviour from individuals or groups. This includes bullying, loneliness, gender choices, being different.
- You will be able to add to or subtract from this list to suit your own teaching.

Evaluation of teaching.
These questions can be asked by teachers, by those who prepare teachers for qualification or indeed anyone concerned with teacher education and ongoing progress.

- How was the lesson designed to meet the goals or objectives?
- Give specific evidence in this lesson that addresses the stated goals or objectives.
- Give evidence, if any, that the teacher used multiple paths to understanding.
- What evidence shows that this lesson was appropriate for these learners?
- What methods did the teacher use to stimulate interest?
- How could this lesson be used to meet external agreed standards of assessment?
- What is the teacher's justification for doing this lesson?

Assessment

- Find evidence that the assessment tool(s) used by the teacher addressed the goals or objectives.
- Were there multiple ways of assessing the learners in this lesson? Give examples.
- What other areas could have been assessed during this lesson?
- Find evidence that this lesson had an impact on learning.

Professional Standards

- What specific standards from your certificate area could be applied to this lesson?
- Are there secondary standards addressed but not discussed in this lesson?
- Find evidence of the use of language from the standards in this exhibit.
- Give evidence that this teacher has knowledge of content.

Reflection

- Could the lesson be adapted for use by others?
- How would you adapt this lesson?
- What other methods of assessment could have been used?
- What strategies used by the teacher could you transfer to your classroom?
- How would you be able to incorporate technology available to you in this lesson?
- Find specific examples in the reflection that addresses what worked well.
- How, if at all, would you do it different next time?

Resources
- List other resources that you are aware of (books, software, etc.) that you could use in this lesson.
- Find evidence of collaboration with colleagues, parents, community or other people in this lesson.

Question types and how to write them
Types of test
Before writing a test it is essential to think about what you want to test and what its purpose is. We make a distinction here between proficiency tests, achievement tests, diagnostic tests and prognostic tests.

- A proficiency test is one that measures a candidates overall ability in a language, it isn't related to a specific course.
- An achievement test on the other hand tests the learners' knowledge of the material that has been taught on a course.
- A diagnostic test highlights the strong and weak points that a learner may have in a particular area.
- A prognostic test attempts to predict how a learner will perform on a course.

Types of questions
- Testing factual knowledge
- True/False
- Yes/No
- Gap-filling
- Matching
- Multiple choice
- Transformation
- Open and closed questions
- Error correction
- Other question types

Testing factual knowledge
Knowledge of facts can be tested in many ways. They do not have to be memory tests. Faced with a text, a learner has to answer a few or many factual questions, most of which will be amenable to short answers.

BREATHING

Our lungs are in our chest, which is the upper part of the body. The lungs are like a pair of balloons. When we breathe, we pump air in and out of our lungs. We take in air containing oxygen, a gas that the body needs. We get rid of carbon dioxide, a waste gas. Because our lungs are always working, even when we are asleep, they need to be very strong. Although they are like balloons, it would not be healthy if they burst easily under pressure.

> How many lungs do we have?
> Where in the body are they found?
> How do gases get in and out of the lungs?
> Why is carbon dioxide breathed out?
> In which important way are lungs different from balloons?

True/false questions

These are easy to write. They can be used for testing of knowledge, or to make learners think more closely about something.

Read the passage about manganese carefully, and then decide which statements are *true* and which are *false*.

> Manganese is always grey in colour.
> Manganese is never found by itself in the earth.
> Plants need manganese in order to grow.
> Some animals do not need manganese.
> If we take too much manganese we can become sick.
> It is impossible to melt manganese.

Read the passage about John Tembo, taken from the novel *Dead Men Don't Talk*, and then choose **five** *true* statements and **five** *false* statements.

1. Tembo was hiding among rocks.
2. Dust was caused by the speed of the vehicles.
3. Tembo guessed his enemy would expect a trap.
4. Tembo had hired three men to kill for him.
5. The two men thought they saw Tembo standing by the car.
6. Sinyanga was hiding under blankets and carried a machine gun.

7. Tembo was certain Sinyanga had become mad.
8. Sinyanga fired many bullets at the standing figure.
9. Tembo's clothes and flesh were torn by the bullets fired at him.
10. Sinyanga did not fear Tembo.

Yes/No questions

Like True/False questions these can be useful for testing factual comprehension.

Did Vasco da Gama sail round the Cape of Good Hope?

Did Henry the Navigator reach India?

They can be useful in grammar tests, too; in the writing of short dialogues to exemplify a point.

A: Are you from around here?

B: Yes, I am.

A: Do you come here often?

B: Yes, I do.

A: Can I buy you a drink?

B: No, thanks.

A: Are you married?

B: Yes, I am.

A: Is your husband here too?

B: Yes, and here he comes now.

Gap-filling questions

A gap filling exercise – often known as a cloze or cloze deletion test – is an exercise that can be used in testing and assessment. A sentence or larger piece of text is presented with words or phrases omitted. Completion can be with a single word – a name, perhaps, or a verb – or a phrase.

Muhammad Ali will always be _____ for his speed when boxing.
1 reminded   2 remained   3 remembered   4 retained

These questions may also be of the type that requires the completion of a sentence. They are used for a variety of reasons, including testing understanding of narrative and causation.

> The thieves chose the supermarket because ....
> Peter was a young boy who...
> The manager was always careful to................................
> The thieves were dressed...

Matching questions

In this question type items have to be matched with others. The questions vary a lot. Because they have an element of a game, they are particularly liked by primary school learners. Many lexical and grammatical items can be tested by matching. The exercise is usually set out in two columns, but this is not strictly always necessary.

tall	old
fair	short
bright	dark
slim	dull
young	fat

Multiple-choice questions

In this question type there is a stem and various options to choose from. One advantage of these questions is that they compel the learner to think carefully before making a choice. It is usual, but not mandatory, to have four choices. Two are incorrect; one is a plausible distracter; and the fourth is the correct answer.

Teachers at all levels favour multiple-choice questions because they cut down on guessing – unlike true/false or yes/no questions – and because they are very easy to mark. Indeed, in external examinations they can be marked by placing an answer template over a sheet. In some cases they can also be marked by machines.

The great disadvantage of multiple-choice questions is that they are difficult to write. Any benefit from the ease of marking is very soon negated by the length of time spent finding viable alternatives which are wrong but not ridiculous. In fact, you will often find examples which are ridiculous, even as a joke, and those are best framed as straight choices in an *either/or* fashion. There is another difficulty, too. There is a lot to read through before choices can be considered. This does not of itself invalidate multiple-choice questions as a tool, but it means time used in reading might be better spent. If we are testing knowledge levels, let us do that, and not test reading skills.

If, despite these caveats, you still decide to write your own multiple-choice questions, it will be useful to bear the following points in mind.

- Know clearly what you intend to test;
- Be clear about the objectives of the test;
- Frame questions in hierarchical order;
- Choose plausible distracters;
- Do not signal the correct answer in any way;
- Always avoid an alternative that states, 'All of the above';
- Avoid adverbs such as mainly, usually, generally, etc, as these questions lack exactness.

Try to anchor your questions within a passage – oral or written, but usually the latter – and avoid asking for opinions. These can be dealt with in other, better ways. Multiple-choice questions are best if it is remembered they are meant to be objective tests.

Examples of multiple-choice questions follow. Whether they are well framed or poorly framed, you can decide.

1. Mr Smith collected money from the tills at 5 o'clock because
   a. he was ready to close the supermarket
   b. he could take the money out by the back door
   c. he was a man of regular habits
   d. he did not trust members of staff

2. The third state to join the American union in 1787 was
   a. New Cardigan
   b. New Jumper
   c. New Sweater
   d. New Jersey

(This question is an actual example from the television show *Who Wants to be a Millionaire?* Whether it was for a hundred or a million, we have not bothered to check. If four true examples were given – there are four American states all called New – it would be a tough question, but not beyond anyone with a knowledge of American history and politics of the 18th century.)

3.   Trade unions were formed because workers needed to
    a.   resist powerful organizations dominated by employers
    b.   advance their struggle for political rights
    c.   get together to discuss common interests
    d.   improve their working conditions

In writing the stem of the question it is best to avoid repetition, as there would be if this third example had the stem: *Trade unions were formed because . . .* and then the four choice all began with *needed to*.

It is worth remembering that multiple-choice questions can be used in all subject areas and at all levels.

Transformation questions

This type of question developed out of a theory of grammar, and such theories are not always the best point of origin for questions. The theory, of how grammatical knowledge is generated and represented, and processed in the brain, was developed by Noam Chomsky, an American linguistics teacher. Chomsky theorized that transformational grammar consisted of two levels of representation of the structure of sentences:

1.   an underlying form termed *deep structure*, and the actual form of the sentence produced, called *surface structu*re;
2.   a system of formal rules specifying how deep structures are to be transformed into surface structures.

Consider the two sentences *Steven wrote a book on animals* and *A book on animals was written by Steven*. According to Chomsky there is a deeper grammatical structure from which both sentences are derived.

This transformational grammar theory formed the basis for many subsequent theories of human grammatical knowledge. Since Chomsky's original presentation, many different theories have emerged. Although current theories differ significantly from the original, the notion of a transformation remains a central element in most models. In textbooks, the result has usually been exercises based on the use of active and passive moods in writing sentences. It is our contention that this examination of grammar, and exercises pertaining to it, is better left to linguistics departments in universities, where it has interest and value. Used in primary and secondary school textbooks, the result is the generation of mechanical writing tests better taught and tested elsewhere in the programme.

Open and closed questions

These are two types of questions are different, not least in their usage. A closed question can be answered with either a single word or a short phrase. How old are you? and Where do you live? are closed questions. Yes/no questions are closed. When Macbeth asked, in the famous soliloquy, *Is this a dagger I see before me/The handle toward my hand*? he was asking himself a closed question.

If, on the other hand, you ask someone the state of their health, even if you can safely predict the answer, that is an open question.

As a general rule – and clearly you will know of exceptions – questions starting with *how*, *are* and *do* are closed questions, generating yes or no answers. Questions starting with 'what', 'where', 'which', 'who' and 'when', are open questions, which require fuller answers.

Closed questions have the following characteristics:

- They give you facts.
- They are easy to answer.
- They are quick to answer.
- They allow the questioner to maintain control.

This makes closed questions useful in several situations, including:

- Initiating a conversation, especially with a stranger.
- This explains why, not least for the British, closed questions about the weather are useful.
- When asking questions without invading privacy.

It's lovely weather today, isn't it?
Try being contrary and say how wonderful it is when the rain is pouring down, and note the reception you get.

- When testing understanding.
    Columbus reached land in 1492, didn't he?
- For setting up a positive (or negative) frame of mind.
    Would you like us to replace your present supplier and do a better job?

You can't really be happy with your present gas supplier's bills, can you?

Are you getting enough money for the job?

You are satisfied with your current teachers, aren't you?

- For achieving closure.

  If I guarantee delivery tomorrow, will you sign the contract now?

Salesmen often find this a useful ploy

Question tags – *isn't it? don't you?* – which imply agreement, can turn an opinion into a closed question. *Surely, you don't want Farmer Jones back, do you?*

Open questions

These are likely to receive a longer answer than a closed question. Although any question can receive a long answer – depending on who is doing the answering – open questions deliberately seek longer answers, and are the opposite of closed questions.

Open questions have the following characteristics:

- they invite the respondent to think and reflect;
- they admit of answers with *opinions* and *feelings.*
- they hand control of the conversation to the respondent.
- Open questions are useful in the following situations:
- To find out more about a person – their individual interests, needs, wants.

  What's causing your insomnia, do you think?

  Why is going out every evening so important to you?

  What prevents you completing your assignments on time?

- To open up a closed conversation and develop it.

  So tell me, what factors keep you focused on your studies?

  What activities interested you on your holiday?

- To explore with someone a solution to their perceived problems.

  You were always punctual to class. What happened to change that?

- By producing positive feelings in people after a time of difficulty.

     How have you felt since your results started to improve?

     How have you been since our last meeting?

Discussions

The technique of learning by discussion is, like the lecture method, an old one, dating back many centuries. Discussion can be called by many names, of which seminar seems to be the one currently favoured. Tutorial group appears to be going out of fashion.

Fashions and styles are not important; successful learning is.

Discussion methods have, as you would expect, both advantages and disadvantages. Before discussing these in more detail, it needs to be made clear that *discussion* and *conversation* are not synonymous terms. Conversations, especially those with like-minded friends and colleagues, are among the most enjoyable activities of one's life, allowing for humour, digressions, going off at a tangent, or whatever. Discussions are more focused, and successful ones address certain topics and the teacher expects and plans for particular outcomes. That said, a discussion need not be boring and concentrate narrowly on a single theme or subject. Properly planned for, discussions can be interesting, creative and even dynamic.

Success in discussions, like any other teaching technique, stems directly from planning. For a teacher to enter a tutorial group and ask, *'Now what do you want to discuss?'* or *'What shall we talk about today?'* – and we have heard both questions more times than is good for our digestion – does not augur well for interest or learning. The teacher may well enter the room and start asking questions; successful teachers often do that. The teacher may well not even mention the topic for discussion but arouse interest by questions and observations. At some early stage, of course, there will be mention of the objectives of the discussion, and perhaps even of the outcomes the teacher has planned for, though the second of these could well inhibit discussion of a creative and dynamic kind. Whether the planned outcomes are stated explicitly or are left until the session's end, and a summary, the teacher should have planned for certain outcomes.

Discussion ought to lead to a number of desirable outcomes, including the following:

- An increase in curiosity about a topic, leading to learning;
- Positive perceptions arising from the discussion;
- Increased amounts of time spent reading about the subject under discussion. If the teacher has announced the topic in advance, the reading might have been done earlier than the discussion period. If not, increased levels of interest should motivate the learner to further study, or even further discussion with peers;

There must be a purpose or purposes to a discussion. Without a goal, a discussion becomes a conversation, and probably lacks the verve and interest of a successful conversation.

Teachers often consider discussion to be a waste of time, and if the teacher is not in control, a rowdy waste of time.

We remember a head teacher stating in a staff meeting that when he walked past a classroom, which he did often, he wanted to see the learners with their heads down, writing. That, he asserted, was the one sure way of ensuring discipline in class. Mr Gradgrind and Wackford Squeers were his heroes and mentors. You may not be entirely surprised to know that this head teacher was promoted to be a senior inspector.

Before considering teacher attitudes and comments regarding the disadvantages of discussions, it behoves us to be positive and consider the many advantages, as we see them.

1. all members of the group, including the teacher, are able to contribute;
2. because discussions are enjoyable, they are motivating activities;
3. the nature of discussion is democratic;
4. therefore, learners can become successful and democratic in their own areas, whether as teachers, engineers, doctors or whatever;

5. there can be clarification of facts or of problems;
6. new explorations can be introduced into the discussion at appropriate times;
7. the teacher is able to gauge the understanding and opinions of learners and this is useful feedback assisting future lesson plans;
8. the teacher can at the end present a summary of opinions, and perhaps lead the group toward consensus.

Notwithstanding these **eight** persuasive points, many teachers question the efficacy of discussions. We understand the points made, even when we do not necessarily agree. It is certainly true that some people are by nature and character more successful than others as leaders of discussions. That, by itself, is no good reason to neglect what is a useful learning tool. Among the arguments stating the disadvantages of the technique are

- unless the topic or discussion has interest for the learners, there will be a lack of participation;
- some participants dominate the discussion;
- others become resentful of this dominance and are reluctant to participate;
- if the leader of the discussion is not strong enough, or lacks focus, the discussion deteriorates into a confrontational argument rather than an exercise in democracy;
- discussions go off on tangents and cannot always be returned to the topic intended
- when one learner is answering or asking a question or making a point, other are often disengaged, especially if the speaker is not liked for any reason;
- pacing is a problem, because learners think and process ideas at different rates.

For these reasons, participants seem bored during discussions and look as if they are eager for the bell to end the session. Such boredom too often leads to absenteeism, especially at the tertiary level of education.

So what can teachers do in order to continue with discussions and yet get rid of the disadvantages?

Begin with the matter of questions. Before a session, construct questions related to the topics that are at different levels and understand each level, whether

- high level
- divergent
- structured
- simple

Asking a well-formed question does not always guarantee that the question will elicit a response. It is necessary to decide how long to wait for an answer. Fearful of losing momentum, teachers usually provide an answer within three seconds of asking a question. Some teachers do not even pause, and answer immediately, even though the question they asked was not intended as a rhetorical question. Either way, there is no chance that learners will be able to offer an answer. A complex question requires a lengthy waiting time. The teacher should silently count to about ten, or even fifteen, and then, if the silence persists, interrupt and offer assistance. But long waiting periods can lead to an increase in tension, or allow the unpopular loud member of the group to dominate once again. It is suggested that after ten seconds the teacher needs to state the question in another form, allowing for clarification or simplification. Alternatively the teacher can, as part of the question say

- Take your time in answering this question.
- Consider carefully before you answer.
- Give this question a minute before you answer.

The teacher should not resolve the tension by looking closely at a particular member of the group, at least not one known to be usually dominant.

The framing of questions is important too. Because this is a discussion session, it does not follow that all questions need to be oral. This sometimes results in questions not being understood or even heard fully. A resolution to the difficulty may come from the teacher writing the question

- on the chalk board;
- a flip chart;
- or writing down and copying before the session.

The third option allows for prior discussion of how far the questions are understood. Generally speaking, however, the answer is in having small groups and, where necessary, writing a question on the board or chart. Nothing should be allowed to interfere with the flow of discussion.

Learners are active when they are engaged in thinking about or discussing issues that interest them. This can mean issues relevant to a course or a text, and need not merely refer to personal or social issues. Therefore, teachers should strive to maximize learner activation, as well as participation. It could well be that an answer is to divide a large class or group into smaller groups, which will increase individual activation. This is a teacher technique to be discussed later. For now it is relevant to mention that a teacher can begin with a plenary session and then divide the larger group into smaller groups. This is a successful technique in many areas, and not merely in education institutions.

Success or failure in discussion groups depends almost entirely on the level of teacher preparation and on control of the discussion. The quality of leadership is vital. Too many teachers never look beyond the learners at the front. We have noticed this in many classes we have observed. If a learner cannot catch the teacher's eye, there is certain to be inhibition and eventual loss of interest. So all members of the group should be encouraged to participate. Comments such as:

'That's an interesting point. Do you agree, Karen, or disagree? Perhaps you can tell us"
'James, I can see you shaking your head. Perhaps you'd like to tell us why.'

In such ways the teacher not only encourages participation by all, and subsequent activation, but also reinforces participation on a continuous basis and in a variety of direct and indirect ways. On the other hand, those who are active in discussion, or seek to dominate, must be dealt with tactfully. Comments can be made in front of the whole group, or privately afterwards. With the former, comments such as:

'That's a valid point, Peter, but let's hear what others have to say on this topic.

'I wonder if everyone agrees with that, Peter. Let's hear what Mike has to say, shall we?'

Many teachers, especially younger ones who have been taught in this way, now begin a lesson or session with an *ice-breaker*. These are valid and useful, so long as they do not embarrass participants, as some of the sillier ones do. Teaching is not music hall or vaudeville. An ice-breaker should have an educational purpose and be allied to the topic under discussion.

When the discussion finishes, that is not the true end for the teacher. There is a need to evaluate what has occurred, and how far objectives were met. It is useful to have a sheet for completion. This will not take up too much of your valuable time. It allows you to plan for the next discussion, and how to improve in certain perceived weak areas. On your sheet there should be the following:

- The major point(s) discussed;
- The conclusions at the end of the discussion;
- Outstanding points for resolution;
- What was accomplished;
- The attitudes discussed;
- Feelings expressed in the discussion;
- Names of any dominant participants;
- Names of any non-participating learners;
- Points for planning the next discussion session.

Work in pairs

Working in pairs is currently a popular teaching method. It is also, of course, a method often used in offices, factories, hospitals and other places of work. There are many good reasons why people like to work with another person, but this must not be taken to mean that everybody enjoys working with another person, or finds it better or more productive than working alone.

There is a common belief that planning to teach a whole class is less democratic than it ought to be, and that using pair work or group work is one way of ensuring that learners are being prepared for participation in a democratic society. This is not the place to argue this contention, one way or the other. What matters is that we discuss how teachers – who are likely to want to use pair work, or have it impressed on them that they *ought* to use it – are able to plan in ways that they make the method effective.

Working in pairs means two learners working together collaboratively. It most assuredly does not mean two people working separately and then pooling their ideas, so that they only do half the work. That said, when two people are together, whether in a learning situation or not, it will very soon become apparent that one is more assertive than the other. To borrow a comparison from rally driving, one is the driver and the other is the navigator. There is a role for both to play. In many situations, not excluding classrooms, these roles are not complementary; one person is making most, if not all, the decisions. What is more, one person will be happy to assume the secondary or dependent role, and, such is human nature, there is never a shortage of people anxious to be the dominant one, whether it is two children in a primary school or two politicians working for election victory.

Planning for pair work is always accompanied by doubts, and these are often about the value and the disadvantages of using this method. Disadvantages may be real or perceived. What has been noted, in many situations, is that working in pairs does not always reduce the amount of work needed to be done. In fact, anyone who has been accompanied by a trainee teacher knows that having to explain, observe and then follow up is more onerous than teaching by oneself. This is not to suggest that trainee teachers should not be helped – that would be nonsense – but it does show that working in pairs is not always the most effective method in a situation.

A second objection to pair work is that individuals need time and space of their own in order to work. This cannot be denied and it would be foolish if learners undertook pair work to the exclusion of other methods.

There is also the objection that one learner is using another, perhaps a brighter one, in order to learn. This cannot be a genuine objection. From time immemorial, people have worked and learned in pairs. It is the very centre of the apprentice system, where a tyro learns from an experienced person. In an industrial or company context, knowledge transfer happens and the company benefits from dispersing knowledge among all staff.

In schools – and in society as a whole, of course – the two persons may have dissimilar backgrounds. Unless there is a deep-rooted prejudice, this should not present problems, and where a prejudice exists, teachers should be able to deal with it. In fact, by putting together two learners of dissimilar background may well be a tactic to lessen the prejudice.

The matter of assertiveness is something that teachers, at whatever level, observe every working day. It is argued that work in pairs increases dialogue between the two. Indeed, noise levels do usually rise during this kind of activity. Noise levels do not relate to learning. Levels of assertiveness definitely do. This would seem to run counter to the intuitive notion that low assertive learners should be paired with more highly assertive ones in order to keep discussion going, and that the more assertive learner will help the less assertive one. Intuition is never as good a guide as observation. Nor does it follow, as observation again shows, that a less assertive learner is likely to be weaker than the other. There does not appear to be any correlation between levels of intelligence and levels of assertiveness.

Some teachers rarely use pair work – or group work for that matter – because they fear losing control of a class. The answer is: to gain control, through a variety of tactics, and then introduce pair work. There will be talk. Noise levels will rise. Teachers need to inform learners that if noise levels rise too high, there will be a signal. This could be the teacher clapping hands, striking a desk with a ruler or something similar. What is not recommended is for the teacher to attempt to shout above the noise, thus making it worse. Of course, there is no reason why several pairs talking should be noise. If there is argument and dispute, the teacher can step in to offer advice and correction.

We are committed to the use of pair work in class. Advantages include

- learners have more speaking time – this is especially needed in language classes, not least those learning English as a second or foreign language;
- opportunities for learners to practise pre-written dialogues illustrating a lexical or grammatical point;

- changing the pace of a lesson − work in pairs should never take up the whole time allotted to a period of learning;
- placing the learners at the centre of learning processes, with the teacher acting as facilitator;
- by changing pairs round regularly, learners are able to interact with everyone in the class.

When planning for pair work take care to

- explain your procedures in advance;
- state what the objectives are;
- stress the value of such work, even in a primary school;
- have clear rules for learner movement
- demonstrate with a learner − or possibly a teaching assistant − how it should be done;
- have a set time for the activity;
- give feedback to the whole class, and state if you think the objectives were met and, if not, explore why that might be so.

Situations which lend themselves to pair work
- Using the telephone;
- Going to the bank;
- Eating in restaurants;
- Purchasing tickets: at the cinema, for the theatre, for a concert;
- Visiting the doctor or going to the hospital;
- Visiting the public library.

Why not include the supermarket, you may ask. We have noticed that it is possible to purchase items from a supermarket and the only words spoken are you saying *thank you*. Don't expect a dialogue in a supermarket. Here is one that actually happened.

SELF   Thank you. (*Pause*) Haven't you been trained to say *please* and *thank you?*
CHECK OUT   It's on the receipt.

We checked and there, sure enough, were the two words and the hope we would come again. We never have.

Group work

Many of the points made about work in pairs apply also to group work. This is particularly true of teachers' fears that such work leads to rowdiness and possible lack of control.

Planning for group work

In order to prepare for group work, the teacher will need to do the following:

1. prepare any physical materials for group work ahead of time;
2. anticipate the size and the selection of groups;
3. anticipate how learners will be organized within the groups (tasks and roles);
4. consider the timing of the group work;
5. consider how the small group work will be shared with the entire class and linked with the overall curriculum.

Selection of tasks

There are multiple tasks that can be shared among group members or a single task that benefits from participation by all individuals within a group. Selection of the activity is important, of course. An activity that is best suited for group work will probably meet the following criteria

- The task will involve problem solving;
- The task will involve specific discussion;
- The task will use materials of various kinds;
- The task will be best completed through the development of ideas or arguments.

Preparation of materials

The teacher will need to organize learners to collect materials and physical specimens for investigation.

Size of a group

A group will normally consist of four learners, but three people are acceptable, five is probably too many, especially in the classroom or laboratory. One member of the group will be chosen, by teacher or learners, to act as 'secretary' if it is necessary, as it often will be, to make a report of the group's activities and conclusions to the whole class. It is not recommended that any individual be named as group 'leader.'

Selection of members of a group

Group membership can be determined in different ways. In a non-random selection, groups are chosen by the teacher based on prior knowledge. Usually, groups are selected to maximize diversity within the group, since diversity enhances learning. Such groups often have a balance of male and female, and learners with differing ability levels. Teachers can also use their judgement about personality mixes that would enhance the work of the group.

Sometimes groups are organized only for one activity. At other times, teachers use the same small groups for a series of activities, so that learners become accustomed to working with one another. If tables and chairs cannot be moved for group work, then learners, especially young ones, can form groups by turning around in seats to face the children behind.

Timing of group work

The teacher needs to plan ahead and thus anticipate learners' questions about timing. The giving of clear instructions is essential. In many classrooms small group activity constitutes 15 or 20 minutes of period, with 10 minutes allowed for sharing work and conclusions with the whole class. Sharing with the class in oral form is useful but the sharing can also be by putting written results on the walls.

Some teachers, even experienced ones – we could almost say especially experienced ones – consider group work to be a waste of time, a session of aimless chatter interrupting *real* learning. If there is aimless chatter, this is surely the fault of the teacher, for allowing it, for not being clear about objectives, for not preparing tasks adequately.

Group work is a form of cooperation, to be encouraged on social grounds alone. Be democratic in your methods and you are planting seeds for the future. We remember once casting a play based on Alan Paton's novel *Cry, the Beloved Country*. Two male attorneys were needed. Exigencies of casting meant we had to cast a male and a female. Several years later, both learners took law at different universities: the young woman became a respected solicitor, while the young man became a judge. An example of spreading seed and trusting that some will take root in fertile ground. Or, put another way, the law of unintended consequences. Putting on a play is, of course, a good example of group work and cooperation.

Case studies

Origins of case studies

As a distinct approach to teaching, learning and research, use of the case study originated only in the early 20th century. The *Oxford English Dictionary* traces the term *case study* to 1934, after the concept of a *case history* in medicine. A *case* was what doctors called a person until they re-discovered that cases are in fact individuals.

Case studies are used as a teaching method and as part of professional development, especially in medicine, business studies and legal education. Case studies have gained popularity in education and in particular educational evaluation. Case studies have become more popular with teachers for a number of reasons:

- dissatisfaction with the perceived weaknesses of the lecture method;
- the view that the teacher is no longer a fount of knowledge, but a facilitator, and that learners should be allowed to play a part in their own learning,
- because it has been clearly demonstrated in many studies worldwide that learners are able to learn more effectively when actively involved in the learning process.

The case study approach is one way in which such active learning strategies can be implemented. One way of defining a case study could be to say that it is a number of learner-centred activities based on topics that demonstrate theoretical concepts in an applied setting.

A case study is essentially a tool for teaching learners methods of research into a subject. It is not the only method of undertaking research but it a useful one and, if the teacher remains sensible, and does not allow younger learners to go too far out, a manageable one also.

All subjects are amenable to being learned through a case study, and the tool can be used at all levels too; it is simply a matter of adjusting to the age, interests and needs of the learners.

It has also been found that where there is a shortage of textbooks and other printed material case studies are a very useful tool indeed.

The case study is one of several ways of research and learning. Other ways include

- observation;
- experiments;
- analysis of archival information;
- conducting surveys, which may be oral or written.

Case studies are not a substitute for these other methods, they are not alternatives – rather, these other methods can be used within the overall case study. They are not so much a teaching method as a research strategy, to be used with teaching methods. They allow observation, discussion, collection of data, analysis of the data, the formulation of hypotheses and the testing of those hypotheses. In history or social studies, teachers and learners are able to discover what happened, why it happened, how people were affected and what were the results of an event or series of events. Phenomena can be examined within a context that has application to real life, or often contemporary events.

Types of case study

Exploratory
These are usually small-scale and undertaken before a large-scale investigation. In the classroom situation, the exploratory stage will be an integral part of the case study itself. It is important to keep an open mind in these early stages and not rush to conclusions.

Narrative
Findings are presented in a narrative format, usually a drama. This is often done by those studying historical events from a particular ideological standpoint. The results, for some observers, are often neither good drama nor accurate history.

Programme effects
These studies can help to determine the impact of a programmes and provide conclusions about the reasons for success or failure.

Cumulative
These bring together data collected from various studies at different times. They are useful in being able to cut across subject divisions. From the aggregated data it is possible to construct hypotheses and consider future trends.

Embedded
This type is a case study containing more than one sub-unit of analysis. It provides an opportunity to integrate quantitative and qualitative methods into a single research study. The identification of sub-units allows for a more detailed level of inquiry than is usually possible.

Critical instance
These are useful for the examination of one or two issues, with no general conclusions. With younger learners it is best to avoid terms such as critical instance. This case can be used for determining cause and effect, as, for example, with erosion of river banks in environmental studies, the unexpected death of Oliver Cromwell in history, or the effects of economic sanctions on *apartheid* South Africa.

Objections to be overcome
A question to ask yourself is this: will the introduction of case study teaching prove to be a problem for you and for your learners? You can be sure that there will be problems. The good news, however, is that all can be overcome with tact and persuasion.

First of all, you can be sure that some colleagues (especially those long-serving members of staff who are often most resistant to change) will always bridle at the introduction of anything they consider to be novel, or may cause them to be roused from their traditional ways, which they favour because they are sure, beyond a peradventure, that the traditional ways are tried and trusted, and therefore in no need of replacement.

Some will argue, as they did with group work, that case study work is certain to lead to more activity and movement, more discussion, and therefore to higher levels of noise and lack of discipline. This will be a concern from those members of staff who teach in rooms adjoining your own. They may add that maintaining discipline is hard enough as it is, without you adding oil to troubled waters.

It may well be that you have to persuade a head of department or some other manager that what you propose has educational value, and will improve learning. You will probably be asked to write down your thoughts on paper, possibly for discussion later. Do not shy from this request; if nothing else, it will help you to sort out your own reasons for doing case study work. In order to impress these people, who have influence over your teaching and your future preferment, you should mention that research has shown that, far from increasing indiscipline, the higher levels of interest among all learners leads to better control. And you could always add – because it is true and because it always impresses managers – that external examiners such as OfSTED always look kindly upon activities such as case studies when they arrive to undertake their inspection.

All teachers, at whatever level, should encourage active learning, and provide as many opportunities as are feasible and sensible for the development of key skills such as communication, group work and problem solving. Learners who are enjoying a topic, and see sense in the methods being adopted, are sure to have higher interest levels, a greater desire to learn. Most courses already have built into them opportunities for case study teaching. This readily understood in such areas as Business Studies, History and Environmental Studies. Our contention is that all subject areas can be tackled using case study methods.

Teachers ought not to try to hide the fact that case study teaching requires a lot of time for preparation. When actually teaching, the same constraints apply. It has to be admitted that something else may have to be postponed, used less, or be dispensed with altogether. Learners have to be allowed sufficient time for background reading, exploration of research methods and writing down procedures and results. The use of Information and Communication Technology (ICT) is a boon.

Strategies to foster interest among learners
- Choose a subject from the course and make it clear that assessment of the case study will be part of the course;
- Choose a topic from the course that is more likely to interest learners, by allowing them to be part of the process of choosing;

- Ensure there is a wealth of material available for research, whether in written or visual form;
- Invite outside speakers with personal knowledge of the topic: a business manager, perhaps; someone who was a combatant in a war; a person from local government; a politician; a retired teacher;
- Arrange outside visits. Properly prepared for, these can be valuable. Costs may be put forward as a means of discouraging you, but be ready with your answers. Explain that a visit to the Victorian museum is essential for practical work and that a particular stretch of river shows erosion patterns seen nowhere else outside the country/region/area.
- Be ready too for questions about health and safety issues, and be able to quote or at least refer to the necessary guidelines, especially if these are part of a school or college policy.

The introduction of key skills into case study work

Individual study skills
Case studies are a good vehicle for encouraging learners to carry out independent research outside of the classroom or laboratory.

Information gathering
Case studies require resource investigation and this encourages learners to utilize a number of different resources such as the Internet, school library and the municipal library. Municipal libraries usually have a good collection of local interest material, much of it in the form of posters, handbills, letters and it is possible to scan these or to photocopy them.

Work in pairs
Two people working collaboratively can motivate each other, especially if they are already close friends.

Group work
The benefits of group work, as of working in pairs, have been made clear already. Teachers need to observe closely, to catch signs of dissension within a group, or of some learners become too dominant.

Presentation skills
Most case studies require learners to present work and conclusions in a variety of formats. These can be presented

- orally
- visually
- in writing
- as diagrams

Practical skills
Some case studies involve practical work. This depends entirely on the project. If a component element is to develop machinery or a model, it must be demonstrated practically that the machine or models works effectively.

Time management
Case studies require learners to consider how best to carry out the work so that it is completed to the set deadline. A preparatory lecture or class discussion, or both, will prove invaluable in this respect. Can time management be taught? Our answer is that if something can be learned, it ought to be possible to reach it.

A lesson plan for a case study project will include the following items:

Case Study
Length
Level
Course
Number in class
Objectives
Key Skills
    Presentational skills
    orally
    visually
    in writing
    as diagrams
    Group work skills
    Time management
Assessment strategies

Project work

Project work as a teaching approach offers the opportunity to create learning environments which, if not innovative – for nothing is ever new – are at least varied. Learners are given opportunities to

- work in groups, learning team and collaborative skills;
- engage in a variety of meaningful activities, such as:
  o seeking solutions to problems
  o engaging in analysis
  o finding the best way to present work
  o suggesting appropriate ways of evaluating findings;

Project work has, clearly, much in common with case study work, and it would be pointless to repeat all points regarding advantages and disadvantages. It is worth pointing out, however, that increased motivation is usually a result of projects carefully prepared. In addition, learners have to use a variety of skills, of which the most important, perhaps – not least for those learning English as a foreign or second language – is the need to use the four skills of listening, speaking, reading and writing.

Tasks have end products, whether in tangible or intangible form, but usually the former. Tasks are authentic and authenticity is important, especially where learning is job related, as increasingly it is. The end products can be displayed

- for view by the whole class;
- others in the school or college;
- or by parents and other interested adults at open evenings and the like.

Such display is also a motivating factor.

Project work is a series of coordinated learning experiences. It is useful in allowing learners to bring to the project skills and experience learned in other places. This provides opportunities for synthesis and reference to real life situations, which is far from true in a great deal of instruction that still takes place in far too many classes. This is not to argue that all learning should be job-related; that is the philistine's conclusion. Nevertheless, it is an admission that learning is about meeting the challenges of maturation; that learning is for life, and should have continuing relevance throughout life. It sounds like a paradox, but working collaboratively in groups assists an individual learner on the path to independent learning.

Role playing

This section is not about drama in education. While there are, unavoidably, certain points where drama and role play overlap, our concern is with the uses and advantages of role playing in courses other than drama courses. There are challenges and difficulties, and these will not be shirked.

We are happy to raise our standard immediately: we believe that role playing has value in education, at all levels – it is not simply for little children in primary classes. But like all methods it should not be used too often, lest familiarity lends itself to boredom and contempt. Nor should it be considered a standby for a wet Friday afternoon, entered into without thought and preparation, though, given the right preparation, Friday afternoon might well be the best part of the week for it. All teaching, whatever the method, has to be approached with forethought, planning and research. This applies equally to role playing in education.

It is essential to understand that this section deals with role play in education and not with play generally. It is being argued in several places – for example, an article by Sarah Harris, education correspondent of the London *Daily Mail* 30.05.06, under the title *Are children being deprived of play skills by parents?* – that natural creativity is being stifled by hi-tech toys, fears for safety if children attempt certain activities, and lack of adequate spaces for play. Regimented play activities can have negative consequences on the social and emotional development of a child, Harris writes, 'because they are too organized and take away a child's initiative and freedom of choice. In contrast, freeform play encourages the creative and multi-sensory development of a child because it has no structure.' The teacher is planning for role playing and not for play, and structure is essential.

By this time it will be clear to readers that not only are there points of overlap between drama and role playing, but there are points of overlap between all classroom teaching methods. This is inevitable, as methods are only placed in different sections as a means of bringing order to the subject. It is hoped that by now the larger picture is becoming more evident, the pieces of the jig-saw puzzle falling into place.

What are the uses of role-playing?

Motivating learners

Role playing is generally fun for learners, as it presents opportunities to imagine themselves as someone else, and has within it the elements that are social and creative. There is also an element of competitiveness. While many teachers wish to eliminate competition from their teaching, as from groups and even society as a whole, in the cause of social engineering, learners all too often frustrate these attempts by exhibiting fiercely competitive streaks of behaviour. This is not the place to debate the topic, nor would we be so foolish as to espouse extreme social Darwinist views, but there is much evidence to suggest strongly that human beings – like most organisms – have progressed through a mixture of competition and mutual aid.

Learner-centred activities

Properly organised and planned for, role playing is learner-centred, open-ended, and can be made to deal with events and issues that are closer to real life situations than lectures and other more formal methods of teaching.

Interactive learning

Interacting with individuals playing a part, or small groups, is good preparation for other learning activities involving interactions. It is also a means to introduce learners to real-life situations, though this should never be, perhaps, the central purpose of role playing.

Collaborative learning

Like interactive learning, with which it is closely allied, collaborative learning can assist in problem-solving. There are many examples from most subject areas. In history, questions are asked: Why did the Chartist Movement in England fail? Why were the colonists successful in forming a United States of America? How did it come about that Hitler was not stopped on his road to war? But problem solving can be applied to science, environmental studies, mathematics and most other curriculum areas.

Diagnostic activities
Role playing provides opportunities for assessment on the part of the teacher, and for self-assessment by learners. Both teachers and learners can sometimes discover which areas of the course are presenting problems for individuals or for whole groups.

Real-world skills
Role playing has uses in learning social skills. Cooperation and persuasion, the development of skills such as courtesy, tolerance, managing conflict, understanding the attitudes of others through empathy – not once need the teacher mention these terms, yet they can be embedded within role playing activities.

Debating skills
These skills appear to be in danger of being lost, when models on television employ tactics such as shouting down an opponent, or audiences stamp their feet to ensure that minority opinions are not heard. Teachers are able to maintain standards of civilized debate through role playing. We rate the teaching and development of debating skills very highly.

As with all teaching, so with role playing there have to be the essential components. These are

- a statement of objectives;
- preparation and research, by teacher and learners;
- choice of context;
- choice of roles;
- the role playing activity;
- follow-up discussion;
- assessment.

Like any other activity of this nature, role playing has to be assessed. Where objectives were clearly stated at the outset, its relatively easy to decide – teacher and learners together, perhaps – whether or not the objectives were realized.

When grades are given, they can be allocated for different skills – our old friends listening, speaking, reading and writing – and for such things as levels of cooperation, preparation and execution of allotted tasks.

Successful role playing is where benefits accrue to the learner. A conclusion may be reached, a debate won, a challenger persuaded, even though all recognize that the exercise is a simulation. It is interesting to note that in some case learners enter into the spirit of the exercise so well, that they actually seem to become the character. We recall a debate in which a youth argued an unpopular case so well, and with such skills and fluency, that even his own team started to respond and to attack him with vigour. On this occasion, the youth escaped with no more than verbal threats but where passions are aroused, the teacher needs to be aware of safety issues. Blatner (2002) mentions role playing where power tools were involved. We have conducted role playing exercises where weapons were used, but we ensured that guns and knives were made of wood. Where rules are decided, and followed, with sanctions against those who do not obey the rules, there are not likely to be unexpected outcomes.

The teacher needs to remind learners that peers are also playing a role, and will not necessarily share the opinions and prejudices of their character. To mention this beforehand may well lead to role play that is less than exciting; to discuss it later, may be too late. Perhaps the best method is to have duplicated sheets issued to learners with the ground rules stated clearly. A copy can be pinned to the wall or a board. If nothing else, this will protect the teacher. It is colloquially known as covering one's back, and is as necessary in a learning environment – school, college, university – as in the darkest forest.

Self-directed learning

Several points have become clearer, we trust, as we have explored methods of teaching and learning. One is, that nothing happens by chance: any apparently new method has its roots deep in soil already tilled. Second, the roles and connections between teacher and taught are always evolving, and some reasons for this evolution can be found in changing technologies. Third, and not least important, are the ways in which different philosophies of education – views and notions of what knowledge is, what skills are needed in society and what education is intended for – have always influenced teaching methods. As societies change and evolve, so also opinions on education. Despite what some philosophers and social commentators may have wished to believe in past centuries, not least in the Victorian period, education cannot be divorced from society and its perceived needs, cannot be banished or escape to an ivory tower where learning is pure and disinterested.

What we are calling *self-directed learning* (and no originality is claimed for the term; it is the preferred choice of such pioneers in the field as Roger Hiemstra and Malcolm Knowles) is also known variously as

- autonomous learning
- independent learning
- personal learning
- individualized learning
- experiential learning

These are basically the same; although there are some shades of difference, they need not detain us here. There is also Open Learning, which has a short and honourable history – in the United States, Britain, and, through the University of South Africa (UNISA), in southern Africa too. What all have in common is that they are chiefly directed toward adult learners. We contend that a great deal can be learned from independent learning methods and philosophies and applied, in part at least, much further down the age range, even to primary school classes.

Most adults spend a considerable time acquiring information and learning new skills. The rapidity of change in our world – faster communications, the continuous creation of new knowledge, and an ever-widening access to information – makes such acquisitions necessary. Those who do not use Information and Communication Technology (ICT) soon find themselves left behind in the work place, in schools and colleges, and even in their social life in such matters as purchasing holidays, buying theatre tickets, ordering books online and the myriad of other tasks that many use with ease and facility. Much of this learning takes place at the learner's initiative, even if available through formal settings. Self-directed learning is any form of study in which individuals have primary responsibility for planning, implementing, and even evaluating their efforts and the body of work that arises from those efforts. Most people, whether in a learning environment or a work station – and learning and work take place in both locations – when asked, will proclaim a preference for assuming responsibility whenever possible.

There has been, as the references amply attest, an explosion of interest in self-directed learning, and this interest has been manifested in research papers, conferences, papers in academic journals and even articles in newspapers and magazines. Few topics have received more attention, and one reason is the concurrent development of Information and Communication Technology (ICT). One feeds off the other, in a symbiotic relationship.

But, you may justifiably ask, can models intended originally for adult learners be applied to learners as young as the primary stages? If alterations are made, the age difference taken into account, then the answer is positive. The sooner that learners are introduced to self-learning methods, whether in project work or in case studies, the better will the experiences and skills be gained that allow success further on, until lifelong education becomes something for everyone, or at least available for those who wish to take advantage of what is available. (In this regard, it is to be regretted that in England and Wales the provision of day and evening classes for non-formal learning has been a casualty of perceived needs of cutting costs. That the spending of both central and local government needs to be controlled is not denied; our contention is that education classes, whether job-orientated or for personal development, should be defended. There are other areas where cuts could be made, without any loss to anyone save those in a small and often undeserving minority.)

Self-directed learning has existed for centuries, even back to ancient Greece. It has played an important part in societies where social conditions are not stabilized, and there is a lack of formal educational institutions. Examples are pioneering countries such as colonial America and Australia, where circumstances compelled those who wished to learn to learn on their own, or with at least limited access to others.

Early efforts to understand independent learning include G L Craik in the United States and Samuel Smiles in Britain. However, contemporary interest in independent learning dates back to the 1960s, when the place of people in society consequent on the decline of manufacturing industries in the West, and notions of crumbling hierarchies, were more freely discussed. In the United States, Malcolm Knowles (1913–97) was influential in changing adult educators from the notion of *educating people* to that of *helping people to learn*. This was a significant shift in attitude and thus in choice of methods. In 1975, in *Self-directed Learning*, Malcolm Knowles stated that

- self-directed learning assumes that humans grow in capacity;
- there is therefore a need for self-direction;
- the experiences of learners are a rich resource for learning;
- individuals learn what is required to perform their evolving life tasks;
- natural orientation is task or problem-centred learning;
- self-directed learners are motivated by various internal incentives, which may include
  o a need for self-esteem
  o curiosity
  o a desire to achieve
  o the satisfactions that derive from accomplishment.

David Kolb (b. 1939) is an American educational theorist whose interests and publications focus on experiential learning. In the early 1970s, Kolb explained that the Experiential Learning Model consists of four elements:

1. concrete experience;
2. observation of and reflection on that experience;
3. formation of abstract concepts based on the reflection;
4. testing these new concepts.

The cycle is then repeated. They are a spiral of learning that can begin with any one of the four elements, but typically begins with a concrete experience.

We prefer not to use the term *experiential learning* because it has two contrasting senses. On the one hand the term is used to describe the sort of learning undertaken by learners in institutions, who are offered opportunities, to acquire and apply knowledge, skills and feelings in an immediate and relevant setting. The second type of experiential learning is education that occurs as a direct participation in the events of life. Here learning is not sponsored by some formal educational institution but by people themselves. It is learning that is achieved through reflection upon everyday experience and is the way that most of us do our learning.

Kolb was influenced by Jean Piaget and John Dewey, both important in the development of humanist psychology and education. This is the nub of self-directed learning – that it sees learners as individuals who can and should be autonomous, and thus responsible for their own learning.

Educational institutions at all levels should be considering the following:

- the development of learner independence;
- the implementation of different learning styles;
- the nature of the relationship between teachers, support staff and learners;
- regular review of learning and teaching materials and resources.

Self-learning skills promote learners' abilities in a number of areas. These may have to be taught to begin with. Youngsters do not arrive at school with the skills of recording information or of reviewing and refining that information. Nor do they arrive as blank sheets, with no previous experience. (In fact, they arrive with past experiences and certain abilities that teachers sometimes justifiably wish they had not experienced or attained.) The acquisition of skills encourages independence in problem-solving, decision-making and organization from the very first day in school. Young learners arrive with a natural curiosity, which sensible teachers harness, and others, alas, stifle. No amount of commitment to self-directed leaning can deny the need for teachers to give deliberate teaching. Before learners are able to learn, they must first be given a chance to learn how to learn. Without the many skills required, there can be no independence.

Learners need an environment that is secure and supportive; they must be allowed to make mistakes and feel no shame. The nurturing of skills starts early and is a sustained process. Take one example: once a learners knows how to read a basic story in controlled lexical and grammatical forms is not the end of learning reading skills, but the beginning of a lifelong process. It might be claimed that the job of teachers is to put themselves out of work.

The role of managers in self-directed learning

Managers of schools committed to self-learning policies should ensure that the following are in place:

- a whole-school approach to the development of learning skills
- a consistent approach to skills development by all staff, whether teachers or support staff;
- curricular activities that provide structured opportunities for the development of self-learning skills;
- clear and consistent expectations of learners, with no toleration of slackness.

The role of the learner in self-directed learning

So far we have mentioned that skills need to be developed. Or perhaps we should say, given a chance to develop. How can this be done? And what are the skills that need to be developed? We might also ask, as we are discussing self-learning, what do learners consider to be the skills they need to have for success on self-direction. It would be foolish and utopian, perhaps, to expect young learners to know what is best for them, but it may surprise some teachers – though not those with years of experience, perhaps – just how much learners can participate in the making of decisions about their own learning and how it should proceed.

Specific skills to be acquired might include being able to:

- preview or skim materials before reading them in detail;
- accurately decode and understand written instructions and text;
- summarize the main points of a task;

- use a number of different sources to locate required information for the completion of tasks such as
  - oral resources, including relatives and family friends;
  - resource centres
  - libraries
  - the world-wide web
- plan work schedules;
- predict possible outcomes.

Add to this list being able to:

- study individually;
- work effectively with another learner, as one of a pair;
- co-operate within a small group.

A number of *personal qualities* have to be developed too. These will depend on the individual learner and how they have been raised at home. Among the qualities to be observed and then developed as much as circumstances demand are the ability to be:

- persistent, even in the face of perceived failure;
- realistic in the choice of an assignment;
- organized in the preparation of an assignment;
- skilled in the allocation of time;
- confident in knowing the different kinds of reading;
- confident in knowing the different kinds of writing, especially the making of notes and summaries;
- confident in seeking assistance from others, as required;
- able to transfer skills learned in one area to another, as occasion demands;
- aware that errors are part of the learning process, and something to benefit from.

The role of the teacher in self-directed learning
Teachers need to consult with learners in the setting and clarification of learning objectives, expectations and agreed boundaries of behaviour. Learners need assistance at all levels. The amount of the assistance depends on:

- the age of the learner;
- the understanding of a learner;

- the levels of skills developed by the learner;
- the attitudes of a learner to an assignment;
- the abilities of a learner in cooperative endeavour;
- self-assessment skills.

Learners are unable to learn effectively if necessary *resources* are lacking. This does not merely refer the purchase of textbooks, DVDs and ICT hardware and software. We have successfully taught under trees with no furniture and no text books or similar materials. We have to admit, however, that we were teaching English language skills and could rely on oral work. What it means is access to a wide variety of sources and materials. Managers, advised by teachers as necessary, have to consider that:

- strategies are in place to ensure ready access to resources and resource centres;
- materials are suitable for learner age levels and needs;
- there is a range of materials;
- all departments contribute to the acquisition and development of this range of materials.

Without awareness of these points, a school will be on the way to failing in any commitment to self-directed learning.

Personal Learning Plans (PLP)
A Personal Learning Plan is a document which provides an ongoing record of an individual's learning progress. It belongs to the learner and stay with them throughout their time at school. It remains with them even if the learner moves to a different class, a different teacher, or even a different school. PLPs are used in competence-based education and training, and are a central part of such schemes as NVQs. They are now a part of schools too.

PLPs are a necessary tool to monitor self-directed learning. All those involved in a learner's education – parents, guardian, teachers – have a record of achievement which can be viewed as occasion demands. Teachers are more effective when dealing with someone new if they have a record of past achievement and are thus able to identify future needs. The record goes beyond a subject area and gives a larger portrait of the learner. Crucially, the learner is involved in the programme and makes decisions where it is appropriate for them to do so. In self-directed learning the learner is – to use a term that is familiar nowadays – empowered. There is participation. Personal learning targets, and self-evaluation, are a means of achieving negotiation in learning processes.

Features of personal learning plans

- education is viewed as part of personal development for learning about the world of work;
- a learner is progressively assessed from starting education at school to the day they leave;
- the learner is involved;
- education is not simply a school matter, but takes place in the home and in society;
- there is a focus on personal, social and health education as necessary elements for success in learning;
- study skills and self-directed learning are encouraged;
- there is regular dialogue between learner and teachers.

Other points are included in a PLP but for the moment our concern is with self-directed learning, which a PLP stresses, and which is of benefit to all, if there is commitment by both teachers and the learner. Independent learning habits prepare learners for their place in society as workers and informed citizens. The more each individual learns and internalizes the need for responsibilities at many levels, the better is the health of the nation.

Planning for self-directed learning

As with all other areas of learning, it is necessary for teachers to plan. Such plans may be long-term or short-term. Long-term planning ensures that all areas of the curriculum are covered; that a course has to be covered in its entirety, if at all possible. Short-term planning is similar to what teachers do anyway, which is producing blocks for a set period of time, two weeks (always better for planning than a single week of five days), a month, or half of a semester. There is also the need to prepare an individual plan for a learner. This means more work at the planning stage but eases the load at the teaching stages.

All planning should be effective in terms of time and cost. Tired and exhausted teachers are of no use to learners, or to themselves and their families. Therefore, avoid the duplication of work. ICT makes it easier to be more effective in both these ways. There are teachers still serving who remember the laborious days of writing planning schedules – and work sheets – by hand or on an old upright typewriter that punished fingers to the point of bleeding, and then copying the handwritten or typewritten sheets by means of a spirit duplicator. When photocopiers were introduced, the labour was cut, even though the copier was fed with fluid that marked clothing, and you had to beg the Head's secretary for permission to use it.

In addition, planning should, if it is to achieve success, concentrate on what learners will do in order to learn. What the teacher will do is secondary, though important. Possible outcomes are related to what the learner is expected to achieve, not the processes the teacher will employ to achieve the outcomes. Thus, the focus needs to be clear, identified and related to an objective.

When you present your plans in written or in oral form to managers and colleagues make sure everything is couched in language that is simple to understand by all members of the school, whether teachers or support staff. Extended quotations from Carl Rogers or Roger Hiemstra, and the introduction of terms such as *andragogy* and *autodidaxy*, will impress no one, alienate many and in both cases is unlikely to secure that promotion you and your partner secretly and eagerly covet. Those who care about self-directed learning need to keep as many colleagues as possible favourable to what may to them appear a threat.

Some conclusions regarding self-directed learning
In this process, independent learners develop the values, attitudes, knowledge and skills needed to make responsible decisions and take actions dealing with their own learning.

Self-directed learning is fostered by creating the opportunities and experiences which encourage learners in

- motivation;
- the desire to learn and never stop learning;
- self-confidence;
- self-reliance beyond the immediate learning environment;
- a positive self-concept;

- an understanding of their own interests;
- valuing learning for its own sake.

Self-directed learning is independent, with the degree of independence increasing with maturation. It is part of an ongoing, lifelong process of education that stimulates thoughtfulness and reflection, that promotes the continuing growth of personal capabilities and powers. Learners make meanings about learning for themselves, based on their understanding of why and how new knowledge is related to their own experiences, interests and needs, and perhaps in the fullness of time and maturity they will learn to forge meanings from the apparent chaos of life itself, and come to understand that true reality is multi-faceted, difficult to understand and is not concerned with down-market television shows.

Self-directed learning, therefore, is a direction for the processes of education. There is no absolute standard: each individual is different and each one will use processes with different levels of understanding. This is inevitable because no two individuals are completely alike, not even twins; and subject matter and interests differ accordingly.

Self-directed learning involves teacher and learner in an interactive process that encourages intellectual development, skills development and capacities for independent and reflective judgement. It follows from this that learning environments – schools, colleges, universities – are most likely to contribute to individual success and corporate health where they are flexible, democratic and responsive to the needs and interests of learners. Such an environment strengthens the learner in a variety of ways, all arising from a strong sense of purpose and motivation. It is no mere casual comment to admit that teachers learn a great deal, not only about education processes, the individual learners, but – often to their surprise – about themselves.

The teacher as facilitator

What we have been discussing so far in this section has been the effects on teaching and learning of the cognitive theory known as constructivism. This concept goes back, as we have seen, far into antiquity, with the Socratic dialogue. Socrates attempted by questions to open the minds of his companions and followers. The answers to these questions showed strengths and weaknesses in their thinking, which in turn led to more questions from Socrates. This method of working is still an important tool in teaching and learning.

In the 20th century, John Dewey in the United States of America and Jean Piaget in Europe developed theories of education given the name – often with derision – of *progressive teaching*. The popular notion of progressive schools was an unruly place without order, where learners were out of control and did exactly as they wished, decided which lessons they would attend or skip, and decide what they wanted to learn, if anything at all. This was a gross parody of what to be progressive in education really meant. More recently, because of the theory and practice of Jerome Bruner, David Ausubel, Albert Bandura and others, progressivism has evolved into what is rather clumsily, but correctly, known as *constructivism*. The earlier sections have, in effect, been dealing with this evolution. Now, the rabbit is out of the hat, and constructivism dares to speak its name.

John Dewey wanted education to be grounded in actual experiences. This required study, thought, observation and conclusions firmly grounded in evidence. Piaget believed that we learn by constructing reality for ourselves, building logical structures. Inquiry was what made learning successful. In the Soviet Union, as Russia then was, Lev Vygotsky (1896–1934), a psychologist, in the last ten years of a short life expanded ideas of cognitive development. He emphasized the features in cognition that arise from historical, cultural and social factors, and especially the central role of language. In *Thought and Language* (1934) he defined what he called *the zone of proximal learning*, according to which learners make progress by solving a series of problems; and usually at levels beyond their actual developmental level, but within their level of potential development. And this is achieved under the guidance of parents and teachers, and often by collaborating with their peers. When Bruner introduced curriculum changes he was working from the notion that learning is an active, social process in which learners construct new ideas or concepts based on their current

knowledge within a cultural context. It is somewhat ironical
that the same conclusions were reached in capitalist America and
Marxist Russia, that

- Cognitive development is limited to a certain range at any
  given age;
- Mature cognitive development requires social interaction.

Learning is now recognized as a set of complex processes
involving behaviour patterns in our uses of language in solving
problems.

Psychology has developed rapidly in the last one hundred years
or so. Originally defined as scientific inquiry into the nature of
consciousness, it became with the behaviourists the science of
behaviour. Contemporary definitions include cognitive and emotional elements, as well also biological, social and cultural dimensions.
As interests and focus have changed, so has the language used. As
language has developed, and learning processes have been observed
and described, so has the diversity of theories. Out of the complexity we can distinguish a number of factors that bear directly on
learning and teaching.

- learning is an active process;
- learners order their thinking by ordering their own reality;
- personal activity and the making of decisions is important;
- individual learners cannot be understood without reference
  to the social systems in which they live;
- meaningful and sociallyembedded self-organization reflects a
  developmental flow in which dynamic tensions are essential.

Our lives are a constant process of learning. Order and disorder
co-exist. A dynamic balance between the two is never achieved.
Knowing these things, no teacher ought to be standing in front of
a group for very long propounding knowledge that is apparently
being retrieved from a fact bank and transmitted to the blank slates
called learners. 'It is not just a new horse in a theoretical race. It is
a larger perspective on horses, races and much more.' For the
teacher, the emphases need to be on making connections, seeking
to establish individual meanings, and not simply churning out what
are known as facts. This goes beyond any foolishness concerning
doubt as to whether the battle of Waterloo was fought in 1815, or

whether the Treaty of Utrecht was signed in 1712 or 1713. (The Congress opened in 1712 but individual treaties were not ratified until the following year.) What matters is that the dynamic tensions which are essential for learning have to be allowed, even engineered, for relations between teacher and learner. That means *facilitation*.

But wait! Do not write the teacher out of the script just yet. The teacher is needed, as a guide through the understandings and extended verbal exchanges that take place in classes. Learners may discuss information that was not anticipated by the teacher. That is a product of flexibility. There are no right and wrong answers; dynamic processes, the creation of tensions, are at the heart of what happens. Thus, teachers need to ask questions regularly along the lines of: Why? What do you mean? and What leads you to think that statement is true? In other words, teachers as facilitators challenge the thinking and reasoning of learners. The teacher as the person with all the knowledge, stored away in their heads, proud of that university degree, cannot be sustained in an age of computers. Facts and knowledge are not stored in heads, nor for that matter in computers. Facts are *out there*, available, to be used as occasion demands.

Let us step inside a classroom where the teacher, convinced of the new cognitive approaches of constructivism, is acting as facilitator. The teacher asks questions and poses problems. In fact, the teacher may think they themselves already know the way to solve the problem, and they may well be right; many puzzles, as we know, already have an answer, and our task is to participate in the solving of the problem. Having asked the questions, presented the problem, the teacher now guides learners, discreetly assists them to find their own answers. Such assistance may involve

- prompting learners to ask further questions of their own (inquiry)
- allow for the possibility of more than a single solution to a problem (multiple intelligences)
- encourage work in pairs and small groups – the use of peers as resources (collaborative learning)

The effective teacher never forgets that learners are not blank sheets upon which knowledge is written; they come to learning situations with already formulated knowledge, ideas and understandings. This previous knowledge is the material from which new knowledge will develop. But can this be applied at all levels? The answer is that it can. In a primary school a teacher may ask questions about the ways in which plants and small animals can be preserved. Some learners will already have knowledge of pressing plants. Others will perhaps have knowledge of preserving flesh in formaldehyde. Out of asking questions and posing problems – the amount of equipment to be used; care when handling fluids, especially those considered hazardous. Questions are asked about the effects of low levels of formaldehyde (irritation of the eyes, nose, throat and skin.) It is possible a learner will know that people with asthma may be more sensitive to the effects of inhaled formaldehyde. Learners may be asked to discover what happens if large amounts of formaldehyde are taken by mouth. (severe pain, vomiting, coma and possible death.) It is vitally important, at any level, that enquiry is essential before certain proposals for the solution of a problem are agreed. Dropping a dead hamster in a bucket of formaldehyde will be frowned upon even by the teacher most committed to constructivist theories and practice, just as no sensible parent allows a child to place a hand in a fire in order to justify the enquiry method.

Those caveats allowed, the learner is the person who creates new understanding. The teacher coaches, moderates, suggests, but allows the learners room to experiment, ask questions, try things that do not work, for even failure in scientific enquiry is not really failure at all, but a step along a line of enquiry. Learning activities require the learners' full participation (like hands-on experiments). An important part of the learning process is that learners reflect on, and talk about, their activities. Learners also help set their own goals and means of assessment. Consider this example. In an English language session, the teacher sets aside time each week for a writing laboratory. The emphasis is on content, getting ideas down rather than simply being told and asked to remember grammatical rules. That said, one of the teacher's responsibilities is to ensure that learners have the skills to express themselves well through written language, for much of what is vaunted as free expression is in reality a flow of unpunctuated gibberish, a torrent the teacher needs to stem. In the writing laboratory the teacher provides opportunities for learners to examine drafts from various sources: their own, their peers, even published authors where different drafts are available. Learners take part in the selection and creation of projects. These may include a class magazine. Learners serve as peer editors. With such facilitation the sessions become less like an assignment and more a series of opportunities for learners to value clarity, accepted correct use of writing skills, originality and uniqueness.

Without wishing to labour points already made, facilitation allows learners control of their own learning processes, and they lead the way by reflecting on their experiences. This makes them, by way of gradual stages, creators of their own learning experiences. The teacher helps create situations where the learners feel safe questioning and reflecting on their own processes, either privately or in group discussions. The teacher also creates activities that lead the learner to reflect on prior knowledge and experiences. Talking about what was learned and how it was learned is important. Learning has become, as the language shows, a set of creative processes.

Failure has been mentioned. It is true that learners will discover, sooner or later (preferably sooner, of course) that ideas they had were invalid, incorrect, or insufficient to explain new experiences. If a child is convinced that all trees lose their leaves in Autumn, checking a botany text, a visit to an evergreen plantation, or simply looking outside at a garden in December, will show the conclusion to be invalid. The perceived failure is not important: what matters is that the learner builds on this failure. New knowledge or new skills demand the modification of old understanding. We all know from our own learning that sometimes we may have reached an invalid conclusion that is only changed after many years. We believed that a certain witty quotation was said by Oscar Wilde, and it happens to have been Noel Coward. The earth has not slipped from its axis because we did not have the correct attribution, although we may have lost a couple of points in a pub quiz, and those made the difference between coming first or second. Failure to comprehend the consequences of drinking a bucket of formaldehyde is more serious and fatal than losing a quiz, however, and this is why even those teachers most committed to this kind of facilitation nevertheless lock away toxic substances, and maintain health and safety rules.

Criticisms of the teacher as facilitator

Constructivism has been criticized on various grounds. The first charge against is that it is elitist. This is an unexpected criticism but one that has been stated with vigour from several quarters. Progressive educational theories have been successful with learners from privileged backgrounds who are fortunate in having out-standing teachers, committed parents and rich home environments. Disadvantaged children lack such resources, do not always have committed teachers, and so benefit more from traditional methods using explicit instruction.

A second criticism is that constructivism leads to *group think*. This is an outcome of collaborative aspects of learning. There is, and by the very nature of the strategies used always will be, a tyranny of the majority, in which a few students' voices or interpretations domi-nate the group's conclusions, and dissent is frowned upon or even punished. Yet, as we know from many examples, new devel-opments have arisen from certain individuals refusing to accept the consensus, the accepted view. In the field of cosmology alone, it is necessary only to mention the names of Copernicus, Kepler and Galileo. And when Martin Luther nailed a copy of his *95 Theses* to the door of the castle church in Wittenberg, and unwittingly sparked the Reformation, he did not do so after a discussion with peers.

Another objection is that there is little evidence that facilitating methods work. Critics say that because of the rejection of rigorous evaluation through testing and other external criteria, teachers have made themselves unaccountable for the progress of learners.

It has also been claimed that these facilitating methods have caused learners to fall seriously behind others taught by more tradi-tional methods, and accounts in large part for a general lowering of standards throughout the nation. At the same time the ridiculously high pass rates in certain external examinations – percentages that mirror those found in elections in Soviet Russia and Marxist East Germany – leaves those examination results worthless for employ-ers and for possible or realistic use as predictors in progression to further and higher education.

These are serious criticisms which demand answers, and should not be dismissed as the bleating of traditionalists who would be expected to raise such objections, mainly because they do not understand constructivism, and because change is always accompanied by an element of anxiety.

Our conclusion is this: that in all our teaching – whatever methods or mix of methods are used – there needs to be adequate planning. With planning comes success, and with success there is always satisfaction.

Biographical Appendix

Aristotle (384 BC–322 BC) was a major Greek philosopher, whose work has been influential in Western thought for many centuries and whose work is studied even today. He was a student of Plato and teacher of Alexander the Great. Aristotle studied and wrote on many different subjects: physics, biology, zoology, poetry, theatre, logic, rhetoric, government and politics. He was the first to systematize philosophy and science. His thinking on physics and science had a profound impact on medieval thought, which lasted until the Renaissance. His work has influenced the three major monotheistic religions of Judaism, Christianity and Islam.

David Ausubel (b. 1918) in New York, a follower of Jean Piaget. The central idea in Ausubel's theories is that knowledge is hierarchically organized and that new information becomes meaningful only in reference to what is known already. Ausubel's research has been directed toward intentional, school learning. In this way he differs from behaviourism and cognitive information processing, which attempt to explain aspects of all human learning. Ausubel's theory suggests how teachers can best arrange the conditions that facilitate learning. Ausubel argues that discovery learning, while it may work, is less efficient than other methods. This had led him to research on advance organizers.

Albert Bandura (b. 1925 Alberta, Canada). He studied biology in Canada and then went to the University of Iowa, USA, to study psychology. One of Bandura's research projects studied how people's perceptions of their ability to control what they perceive as threats to themselves affect the release of neuro-transmitters and stress-related hormones into the bloodstream. During this research, concerned mainly with treatment of phobias, Bandura discovered that powerful guided mastery treatment was eliminating snake phobias of long-standing within a few hours in all of the study's participants. The major finding of these investigations was that people can regulate their level of physiological activation through their belief in *self-efficacy*, which is to say their beliefs in their own capabilities. This resulted in the addition of the self-efficacy belief system to social cognitive theory. Bandura developed a conceptual framework that specified the nature, structure and function of efficacy beliefs, the means by which they can be developed, their diverse effects, the cognitive, motivational, affective and choice processes through which they produce their effects, and how this knowledge can be used for personal and social betterment.

Benjamin Bloom (1913–99), born in New York, an American educational psychologist, who led a team at the University of Chicago and has had considerable influence in academic educational psychology. His main contributions to the area of education involved mastery learning and, most notably, his Taxonomy of Educational Objectives in the cognitive domain.

Jerome Bruner (b. 1915) in New York City has been influential in educational theory and practice. His books *The Process of Education* and *Towards a Theory of Instruction* have been widely read and are already recognized as classics. His work on the social studies programme – Man: A Course of Study (MACOS) – in the mid 1960s is a landmark in curriculum development. He has also done research on the connections between education and culture.

Hermann Ebbinghaus (1850–1909) was a German psychologist who pioneered the experimental study of memory, and discovered the forgetting curve and the learning curve. His work on memory, and the techniques he used in research on learning, helped to initiate experimental psychology.

Robert Gagné (1916–2002) was an American educational psychologist best known for his Conditions of Learning. Gagné pioneered instruction for air force pilots in World War 11. Later he developed a series of studies that helped to codify what is now considered to be effective instruction. He also was involved in applying concepts of instructional theory to the design of computer and multimedia based learning.

Roger Hiemstra (b. 1938) is an American psychologist whose interests include: using technology to create adult learning opportunities; identifying teaching implications related to self-directed and distance learning; and discovering ways educators can use community resources to promote learning.

Frederick Herzberg (1923-2000) was a noted American psychologist who became one of the most influential names in business management. He introduced job enrichment and the Motivator-Hygiene theory.

Clark Hull (1884–1952) was born in New York state and became an influential psychologist who sought to explain learning and motivation by scientific laws of behaviour. Hull conducted research demonstrating that his theories could predict and control behaviour. He believed that behaviour was a set of interactions between an individual and their environment and he analysed behaviour from a perspective of biological adaptation.

Malcolm Knowles (1913–97) was born in Montana, USA, and became a leading proponent of US adult education in the second half of the 20th century. In the 1950s he was the Executive Director of the Adult Education Association of the United States of America. He wrote the first major accounts of informal adult education and the history of adult education in the United States. Knowles' attempts to develop a distinctive conceptual basis for adult education and learning became widely discussed. He also wrote popular works on self-direction and on group work. His work was a significant factor in reorienting educators from 'educating people' to 'helping them learn'.

David Kolb (b. 1939) is an American educational theorist whose interests focus on experiential learning, the individual and social change, career development, and executive and professional education.

Abraham Maslow (1908–70), born in New York city, was an American psychologist. He is noted today for his proposal of a hierarchy of human needs and is considered the father of humanistic psychology.

Ivan Pavlov (1849–1936) was a Russian physiologist, psychologist, and physician. He was awarded the Nobel Prize in medicine in 1904 for research relating to the digestive system. Pavlov is widely known for first describing the phenomena of how he was able to train dogs to salivate on command, and from this he developed notions concerning conditioning.

Jean Piaget (1896–1980) was a Swiss philosopher, natural scientist and developmental psychologist. He is well-known for his work studying children and the subsequent theory of cognitive development. Piaget is considered to be the foremost pioneer of constructivist theories of knowing.

B F Skinner (1904–90) was an American who developed theories that learning is a function of change in overt behaviour. These changes are the result of an individual's response to events (stimuli) that occur in the environment. A response produces a consequence such as defining a word, hitting a ball or solving a problem. When a particular Stimulus-Response (S-R) pattern is reinforced (rewarded), the individual is conditioned to respond. The distinctive characteristic of operant conditioning relative to previous forms of behaviourism is that the organism can emit responses instead of only eliciting response due to an external stimulus.

Edward Thorndike (1874–1949) was an American psychologist who spent nearly his entire career at Teachers College, Columbia University. His work on animal behaviour and learning processes led him to the theory of connectionism and helped lay the scientific foundation for modern educational psychology. He also worked on solving industrial problems, such as employee testing.

Lev Vygotsky (1896–1934) born in Belarus (then a part of Russia) and graduated from Moscow State University in 1917. From 1924 to 1934, he did research on cognitive development, particularly the relationship between language and thinking. His writings emphasized the roles of historical, cultural and social factors in cognition and argued that language was the most important symbolic tool provided by society.

John Watson (1878–1958) was an American psychologist who established the psychological school of behaviourism, after doing research on animal behaviour. He is known for having claimed that he could take any 12 healthy infants and, by applying behavioural techniques, create whatever kind of person he desired. He also conducted the controversial *Little Albert* experiment. Later he went on from psychology to become a popular author on child rearing, and an acclaimed contributor to the advertising industry.

Wilhelm Wundt (1832–1920) was a German psychologist and physiologist, and is generally regarded as the father of psychology. In 1879, Wundt founded the first formal laboratory for psychological research at the University of Leipzig, and the first journal for psychological research in 1881.

References

Ausubel, David P. (2000) *The Acquisition and Retention of Knowledge*, Netherlands: Kluwer Academic Publishers.

Ausubel, David P. (1968) *Educational Psychology A Cognitive View*, New York: Holt, Rinehart, and Winston, Inc.

Ausubel, David P. (1963) *The Psychology of Meaningful Learning*, New York: Holt, Rinehart, and Winston, Inc.

Bandura, A. (1997) *Self-efficacy: The Exercise of Control,* New York: W. H. Freeman.

Bandura, A. (1986) *Social Foundations of Thought and Action*, Englewood Cliffs, NJ: Prentice Hall.

Bandura, A. (1977) *Social Learning Theory*, New York: General Learning Press.

Bandura, A. (1973) *Aggression: A Social Learning Analysis,* Englewood Cliffs, NJ: Prentice Hall.

Bandura, A. (1969) *Principles of Behaviour Modification*, New York: Holt, Rinehart & Winston.

Bandura, A. and Walters, R. (1963) *Social Learning and Personality Development*, New York: Holt, Rinehart & Winston.

Bloom, Benjamin S. (1984) *Taxonomy of Educational Objectives*, Boston, MA: Allyn and Bacon.

Bloom, Benjamin S. (1980) *All Our Children Learning*, New York: McGraw-Hill.

Brockett, Ralph G. and Roger Hiemstra (1991) *Self-Direction in Adult Learning*, London: Routledge.

Brockett, Ralph G. and Roger Hiemstra (1985) Bridging the theory-practice gap in self-directed learning in Stephen Brookfield, ed. *Self-Directed Learning: From Theory to Practice*, 31–40. In series New Directions for Continuing Education, Vol. 25. San Francisco, CA: Jossey-Bass.

Bruner, J. (1996) *The Culture of Education*, Cambridge, MA: Harvard University Press.

Bruner, J. (1990) *Acts of Meaning*, Cambridge, MA: Harvard University Press.

Bruner, J. (1986) *Actual Minds, Possible Worlds*, Cambridge, MA: Harvard University Press.

Bruner, J. (1983) *Child's Talk: Learning to Use Language*, New York: Norton.

Bruner, J. (1973) *Going Beyond the Information Given*, New York: Norton.

Bruner, J. (1966) *Toward a Theory of Instruction*, Cambridge, MA: Harvard University Press.

Bruner, J. (1960) *The Process of Education,* Cambridge, MA: Harvard University Press.

Bruner, J., Goodnow, J., and Austin, A. (1956) *A Study of Thinking*, New York: Wiley.

Gagné, R., Briggs, L. and Wager, W. (1992) *Principles of Instructional Design* (Fourth edition), Fort Worth, TX: HBJ College Publishers.

Gagné, R. and Driscoll, M. (1988) *Essentials of Learning for Instruction* (Second edition.), Englewood Cliffs, NJ: Prentice Hall.

Gagné, R. (1987) *Instructional Technology Foundations*, Hillsdale, NJ: Lawrence Erlbaum Associates.

Gagné, R. (1985) *The Conditions of Learning* (Fourth edition), New York: Holt, Rinehart & Winston.

Herzberg, Frederick (1959) *The Motivation to Work*, New York: John Wiley and Sons.

Hull, C. (1943) *Principles of Behaviour*, New York: Appleton-Century-Crofts.

Hull, C. et al. (1940) *Mathematico-Deductive Theory of Rote Learning*, New Haven, NJ: Yale University Press.

Hull, C. (1933) *Hypnosis and Suggestibility: An Experimental Approach*, New York: Appleton-Century-Crofts.

Knowles, M. (1984) *The Adult Learner: A Neglected Species* (Third edition), Houston, TX: Gulf Publishing.

Knowles, M. (1984) *Andragogy in Action*, San Francisco: Jossey-Bass.

Knowles, M. (1975) *Self-Directed Learning*, Chicago: Follet.

Maslow, A. (1971) *The Further Reaches of Human Nature,* New York: Viking.

Maslow, A. (First edition, 1954 and Second edition, 1970) *Motivation and Personality*, New York: Harper.

Maslow, A. (1968) *Toward a Psychology of Being*, New York: Van Nostrand Reinhold.

Miller, N. and Dollard, J. (1941) *Social Learning and Imitation*, New Haven, NJ: Yale University Press.

Piaget, J. (1970) *The Science of Education and the Psychology of the Child*, New York: Grossman.

Piaget, J. (1969) *The Mechanisms of Perception*, London: Routledge & Kegan Paul.

Piaget, J. and Inhelder, B. (1969) *The Psychology of the Child*, New York: Basic Books.

Piaget, J. (1932) *The Moral Judgement of the Child*, New York: Harcourt, Brace Jovanovich.

Piaget, J. (1929) *The Child's Conception of the World*, New York: Harcourt, Brace Jovanovich.

Piaget, J. and Inhelder, B. (1973) *Memory and Intelligence*, New York: Basic Books.

Skinner, B. F. (1971) *Beyond Freedom and Dignity*, New York: Knopf.

Skinner, B. F. (1968) *The Technology of Teaching*, New York: Appleton-Century-Crofts.

Skinner, B. F. (1957) *Verbal Learning*, New York: Appleton-Century-Crofts.

Skinner, B. F. (1953) *Science and Human Behaviour*, New York: Macmillan.

Vygotsky, L. S. (1978) *Mind in Society*, Cambridge, MA: Harvard University Press.

Vygotsky, L. S. (1962) *Thought and Language*, Cambridge, MA: MIT Press.

Watson, J. B. (1930) *Behaviourism*, Chicago: University of Chicago Press.

Watson, J. B. (1919) *Psychology from the Standpoint of a Behaviourist*, Philadelphia: Lippincott.

Wertsch, J. V. (1985) *Cultural Communication, and Cognition: Vygotskian Perspectives*, Cambridge: Cambridge University Press.

Index